1 and 2 Timothy, Titus, and Philemon

by James E. Sargent

General Editor, Lynne M. Deming
Assistant Editor, Margaret Rogers
Copy Processing, Sylvia Marlow
Cover Design by Harriet Bateman

ISBN 0-939697-34-3

Table of Contents

Outline

First Timothy

Second Timothy

Titus

I. Greeting (1:1-4)
II. Commands to Titus (1:5-16)
    A. Regarding ministry and church officials (1:5-9)
    B. A word about opponents (1:10-16)
III. Instructions Concerning Relationships (2:1-15)
    A. Dealing with older men (2:1-2)
    B. Dealing with older women (2:3-5)
    C. Dealing with younger men (2:6-8)
    D. Dealing with salves (2:9-10)
    E. What God expects from all Christians (2:11-15)
IV. Living in Society (3:1-15)
    A. Responsibility to civil authorities (3:1-2)
    B. Reasons/motives for responsibilities (3:3-7)
    C. Another "the saying is sure" (3:8)
    D. What to avoid (3:9-11)
    E. Final personal words and a blessing (3:12-15)

Philemon

I. Introductory Opening (verses 1-3)
II. Thanksgiving (verses 4-7)
III. Paul's Remarkable Request (verses 8-20)
IV. Final Instructions (verses 21-22)
V. Closing Salutations (verses 23-25)

Introduction

Letters are similar to commercials on television. We are aware that some sort of story line has evolved prior to the action and dialogue that we see on the screen. We also understand that specific action continues following the conclusion of our viewing. Letters are similar in that a good deal of drama, relationship, question, and authority all precede the letter. We see only the letter. We are left to our imaginations, unless we have some documentary or legendary evidence, to piece together the results in attitude and behavior that came as a result of the correspondence.

The Circumstances of the Letters

Part of the task of interpretation is placing the letter/correspondence within the context of a relationship between sender and receiver. Real people occupy history. Real people had to make decisions as to how they would live in a real world that, like ours, consisted of conflicting authorities, social demands, personal desires, and anxieties all within a deliberate decision to live life in the context of eternity. Seldom does Paul attempt to present a well-polished, highly refined systematic theology. Teaching or reading the Scriptures requires the skill of imaginative reconstruction. This commentary is written with an appreciation for creative imagination in the task of biblical interpretation.

This commentary will examine four letters. The first three letters, First and Second Timothy and Titus, are letters to younger colleagues in ministry written by Paul regarding church administration. The fourth is the personal letter from the Apostle Paul to Philemon. The great theologian of the thirteenth century, Thomas Aquinas, observed that the first three letters address pastoral concerns. Thus, the letters to Timothy and Titus are commonly called the Pastoral Epistles.

The Shaping of the Canon

Among the critical questions surrounding the Pastoral Epistles are the issues of authorship, date of writing, and audience. A great deal of time and no small amount of scholarly ink have been spent in discussion regarding authorship. As they come to us in the canon, the Pastorals are letters from the Apostle Paul. The reason for this designation is quite clear. The over-arching question that church members asked in those formative days is the same question asked by church members of the modern era: What is the authority of these writings that we should adhere to them?

We will begin, therefore, with a short summary of the shaping of the canon (that is, acceptable books) of the Christian Scriptures.

The process by which a canon emerged began with the ministry and life of Jesus of Nazareth. The oral witness of apostles followed. A crisis of heresy forced the church to make decisions as to what would be acceptable as normative for Christian life and thinking. The canon that emerged from this process has withstood some of the greatest stresses in history. When the church broke into western and eastern branches, the canon (Bible) survived. When the Reformation erupted in Europe, thus splintering Christendom into faction and sect, the canon (Bible) survived. Even in our century with the explosion of religious perspectives the canon (Bible) survives.

Date and Authorship of the Pastorals

We began with the observation that authorship is a critical issue. We have seen that apostolic authorship was essential for a work's inclusion in the canon. But ancient requirements do not dictate developments in study and criticism. Modern scholarship has wrestled with authorship. Essentially three alternatives are possible. One is that the letters were written by the Apostle Paul very late in his life. Much argument can be made to support this perspective, as there is much in the Pastorals that reflects Paul's authentic teaching.

A second alternative is to attribute authorship of the Pastorals to another writer who is familiar with Paul's writing and who uses Paul's name and authority, but who writes to unique circumstances in a much later time. This may sound peculiar to the modern reader, but in ancient times such pseudonymous writing was quite common. For the contemporary reader, however, this format may raise considerable questions regarding the authority of the Bible.

The third option is to search for pieces or fragments of authentic Pauline writing within the Pastoral Epistles. This third option is sometimes called the "fragment thesis," and it discerns five fragments: Titus 3:12-15; 2 Timothy 4:13-15, 20, 21*a*; 2 Timothy 4:16-18; 2 Timothy 4:9-12, 22; 2 Timothy 1:16-18; 3:10ff.; 4:1, 2*a*, 5*b*, 6-8, 18*b*, 19, 21*b*, 22*a*.

This commentary takes the position that the Apostle Paul wrote the Pastoral Epistles. This approach is not an anti-intellectual polemic against scholarly research, nor is it a weak resignation to the impenetrable difficulties of determining exactly who wrote the books. The canon presents the letters to us as Paul's writings. We can imagine the Apostle, who is by his own admission now an old man, speaking to a much younger colleague struggling to work both faithfully and effectively in the missionary enterprise of the new Christian movement.

The Background of the Pastorals

What, then, are the Pastoral Epistles? In short, they are the earliest manual of church order that we possess. During the earliest years of the Christian movement, informal gatherings clustered around the person of Jesus. Later, since by nature human beings order themselves into communities and societies, these gatherings formed the primitive church. The Pastoral Epistles are a concerned pastor's response to the demands made on the leadership of Christian churches as those leaders and the churches live out the life of faith in the midst of the real world on which the author looks with tolerance and acceptance.

One aspect of that world, however, was completely unacceptable. Against the Christian faith there emerged various challenges. These heresies did not come from any single perspective or group. The statements against useless myths and genealogies suggest that the heresies emerged in part from Jewish-Christian traditions. From the Hellenistic/Greek influence came the so-called Gnostic heresies. These heresies were deeply rooted in Greek thought. They included a concern for dualism, a special understanding for only a few who knew more or differently from others, and ethics that were inclined toward the extremely ascetic. To the modern reader this heresy would be akin to the latent danger of a secularization of the Gospel. The final avenue of heresy was the Marcionite heresy, which excluded the Old Testament and helped formulate the New Testament canon.

The Nature of Pastoral Leadership

Throughout the letters the author assumes a developed and reasonably sophisticated church leadership and hierarchy, though the organization of the churches to which Titus is written is not as sophisticated as it is in those to which the letters to Timothy are written. No effort is made to explain how the various functions of church leadership developed. Bishops, elders, presbyters, and deacons all perform the functions of ministry. The leadership is ordained and appointed to various tasks. The details of the various tasks are ignored. Instead, the emphasis is on the character of the pastoral leadership. The selection of officers depends primarily on the moral qualifications of the individual. Under no circumstances should the leader be a new convert.

The leadership at every level must determine what is orthodox and then maintain that orthodoxy in the face of challenges by false doctrine and teachers. Quite clearly the Christian faith developed into a well-formulated body of both thought and practice. No fewer than fifteen references are made to doctrine and/or faith. The church was considered to be *the bulwark of the truth* (1 Timothy 3:15).

Church leadership is to preach tirelessly with careful self-examination so that the preacher will follow the pattern of sound words while guarding the truth. All preachers should handle the truth rightly and set a high example for all to follow. The purpose of the Christian faith is to evoke a high moral standard in followers that is possible only through a thorough knowledge of the Scriptures and adherence to the sound principles of orthodox faith.

The church's leadership is to be a highly disciplined group adequately supported by the balance of the church. Among the specific tasks of clergy are the public worship services of the church and careful protection of the reputation of the church, as well as careful monitoring of doctrines that should and should not be included in those services. Worship services include reading of Scripture, preaching, and teaching as well as recitation of creeds and singing of hymns and doxologies.

1 Timothy 1

Introduction to This Chapter

The Pastoral Epistles, beginning in this first chapter of
Timothy, wrestle with the issue of how a Christian must
be different in theological and ethical awareness, attitude,
and behavior, from the surrounding culture. However,
the Christian cannot remain altogether aloof from culture,
for the Christian does not live in a vacuum. Therefore,
the faith of the earliest Christians is very much like our
contemporary faith, a matter of tension between
specifically Christian identity and generally cultured and
social people.

Paul appropriates a common form of communication
familiar to all in the ancient world. When he could not be
present with congregations or persons he did the next
best thing, he sent a letter via a trusted companion or
fellow worker. Paul's letters have a common structure.

(1) opening
(2) thanksgiving or blessing
(3) body of the letter
(4) specific instructions
(5) closing

Here is an outline of 1 Timothy 1.

 I. Address and Greeting (1:1-2)
II. A Warning Against False Teachers (1:3-20)
    A. The spiritual purpose of the gospel (1:3-11)
    B. Ministry and Christian living (1:12-17)
    C. Real authority and power (1:18-20)

Address and Greeting (1:1-2)

Paul uses the formula first listing the sender, then the addressee's name followed by a brief salutation (see Romans 1:1-7). The letter begins with a strong statement of Paul's authority, *an apostle of Christ Jesus.* Our familiarity with the Scriptures may cause us to overlook the significance of this identity. The writer intends to convey the fact that he does not write merely as a representative of another church. Paul is an apostle by the will of God (see 1 Corinthians 1:1; 2 Corinthians 1:1; Ephesians 1:1; Colossians 1:1; 2 Timothy 1:1). The word *command* carries with it the connotation of a royal command or commission that must be obeyed.

God our Savior is a Jewish phrase (see Deuteronomy 32:15; Psalm 24:5; also Luke 1:47 and Jude 25). Here we see the indebtedness of the Christian faith to its Jewish roots. In the Pastoral Letters the phrase is used frequently as a description of God (see 1 Timothy 2:3; 4:10; Titus 1:3; 2:10; 3:4).

Christ Jesus our hope carries the implication of an eschatological hope. The Christian places great hope not only in this life (see Colossians 1:27), but also in the life to come (see 1 Timothy 6:14).

Timothy is the son of a Greek father and a Jewish mother. Paul first met Timothy during his second missionary journey (see Acts 16:1) in Lystra. He may have become a Christian through the witness and efforts of his mother and grandmother (2 Timothy 1:5). Paul ordained him into the ministry (2 Timothy 1:6).

Timothy is identified as a *true child in the faith.* This may be an allusion to 1 Corinthians 4:17 where Paul characterizes Timothy as his *beloved and faithful child in the Lord.* Philippians 2:19-23 contains warm affection for Timothy. In addition, Paul may also be making an oblique reference to others, the false teachers, who have failed to hold fast to the Christian faith and about whom he is about to speak (1 Timothy 1:3-11; 6:3-10).

In the faith suggests an appropriate emphasis on the spiritual character of Paul's relationship with Timothy. The relationship is based on faith and loyalty to Christ.

In Romans 1:5-7, Paul lists only grace and peace. In Galatians 6:16, peace and mercy are listed. Only here does Paul include all three in a salutation. Some scholars contend that had this been only the work of a different hand, a copier would not have felt the freedom to add to Paul's formula (compare 2 Timothy 1:2; 2 Thessalonians 1:2).

The Spiritual Purpose of the Gospel (1:3-11)

Though Paul mentions a journey to Macedonia, nothing is known about this journey. The journey cannot be fitted into the known journeys in Acts or the accounts of earlier letters. According to some scholars this episode is best fitted into the period after Paul's release from prison.

Macedonia is the Roman province including northern Greece in which are the cities of Philippi, Thessalonica, and Beroea.

Ephesus is a key city in the Christian missionary enterprise.

The instruction to remain may imply the younger colleague's desire to move away from the current stress. Paul gives specific instructions. Timothy is to stand up to all who are preaching and teaching erroneous doctrine. Note that the charge has to do with the nature of the teaching itself and is not yet an exposition on the required character of the teachers. The identity of these false teachers is not revealed at this time. Presumably Timothy as well as Paul would have been aware of specific identity (compare with 1 Corinthians 4:18 where Paul characterizes some teachers as *arrogant*; in 2 Corinthians 10:2 some are characterized as accusing Paul of being too worldly. In Galatians 1:7 Paul refers to unnamed persons who want to *pervert the gospel of Christ*). Evidently these people have not yet reached the deplorable state of spiritual shipwreck of the two people who are named.

The text reads *different doctrine* (RSV) which suggests that the Christian movement had progressed to the point of affirming certain theological formulations. The false teachers dabble in novelties. The terms *myths* and *endless genealogies* suggest a combined Greek and Jewish influence.

The words *divine training* (RSV) may also be translated *God's stewardship*. Paul's concern centers on the message of salvation that has been entrusted to the Christian community. This echoes Paul's concern in 1 Corinthians 9:17 that he not press his own will against the commission with which he has been entrusted. The goal of Bible study is the hearing and holding fast to the message of salvation which can only be apprehended by faith, which is crucial in the steward (1 Timothy 1:1) and in the people taught (1 Timothy 1:4).

The word *steward* evokes the image of a large household. Throughout the Pastoral Epistles the notion of household is central. Indeed, long before church buildings and large membership churches developed, churches were essentially gatherings of Christians in peoples' homes. The image suggests an orderliness within the Christian community that in effect reflects the orderliness of the surrounding culture. Christians shared social values and norms as well as theological understandings.

Paul is not content simply to challenge the false teachers with negative charges. He goes on to describe the positive aims of the Christian faith. The aim of Christian preaching and teaching is love. The Greek term is *agape*. English has but one word, *love*. In the Greek language there are many words to describe different levels or sorts of love . Agape is not a sentimentalized notion of love. Agape is the sort of love expressed through the very character and intention of God.

This sort of love can only be realized by people who are of a pure heart, a good conscience, and sincere faith.

The value of a pure heart is found in the Old Testament (see Genesis 20:5; Job 11:13; Psalm 24:4; 51:10). The heart means more than the source of sentiment. The heart is the center of moral and mental activity. The notion of a good conscience comes from a Greek philosophical background and is often associated with the Stoics. It means an individual is aware of the self but not consumed with guilt or self-reproach. To the Christian it means an individual whose conscience is guided by the will of God and the presence of the Holy Spirit.

The notion of sincere faith may seem foreign to Paul since faith by its nature must be sincere as it is a gift of God. However, Paul is addressing false teachers who are obviously misguided even though they do not realize it. Paul suggests that it is possible to deceive either oneself or others. Such occurrences are not foreign to Paul's own experience. In Galatians 2:13 Paul rues a deception that ensnared even Barnabas.

The false teachers are missing essential qualities. To begin with, they fail to strike (RSV: *swerving from these)* the central aim of agape/love. They end up in futile discussion, foolish talk, or empty chatter. Ironically, these are the same people who claim to be teachers of the law or professors of moral philosophy! Paul summarizes their liabilities. They do not know what they are talking about and are missing the point of the entire Old Testament.

The mention of *teachers of the law* suggests a certain amount of Jewishness in the false teachers. Paul's irony can best be heard if one recalls that the title *teachers of the law* is a title of respect in Acts 5:34.

The mention of the word *law* launches Paul into a digression about the law itself. In sharp contrast to the would-be teachers, Christians understand the law and its limits; the law after all is not the gospel. Perhaps the writer suspected that he had cast aspersions on the law. Here the law is characterized as guidance from a caring God. Recall that in Romans 3:21 Paul avers that the law bears witness to God's righteousness.

Galatians 3:22-23 suggests that there is a universal law which does not need to be laid down for just individuals. This law is only for those who violate the law.

Six general descriptions are listed in verse 9: lawless and insubordinate; impious and sinful; irreligious and the profane. The list of specific wrongdoings follows the order of the Ten Commandments. Patricides and matricides violate the fifth commandment. Murders violate the sixth commandment. Fornicators and homosexuals (that is, sexual vices and/or violators of any kind) violate the seventh commandment. Kidnappers, that is, not trafficking in human beings, but stealing slaves, violate the eighth commandment. Liars and perjurers violate the ninth commandment.

The catalogue concludes with a catchall phrase reminiscent of Romans 13:9 and Galatians 5:21.

In verse 10 the term *sound doctrine* is used for the first time. Other translations for this term include *healthful teaching* or *sound teaching*. The term is used fifteen times in the Pastoral Epistles while only four times in the balance of the New Testament (see 1 Timothy 4:1, 13; 5:17; 2 Timothy 3:16; Titus 2:7).

The Greek word from which we translate *gospel* is *evangelion*. All that has preceded (1 Timothy 1:8-10) is summed up in verse 11.

The used of the word *blessed* is common in Hellenistic Judaism (see 1 Timothy 6:15).

With which I have been entrusted refers to Paul's dramatic encounter with Christ on the road to Damascus (see 1 Corinthians 9:17; Galatians 2:7). The term also suggests a weight of authority. Paul is one of the towering figures in the foundation of the church, and the spiritual father of Timothy. Paul has appointed Timothy to this present duty and has authority to confute false teaching.

Verse 11 serves as a transition from the digression on the law back to the central concern of the gospel.

Ministry and Christian Living (1:12-17)

Autobiographical reflections form the backdrop against which Paul's authority must be seen. Paul's ministry is the result of nothing less than Christ Jesus, who apprehended him on the Damascus road. Paul's ministry is the direct result of an appointment by Christ. Paul echoes the earlier mention of *entrust* (1 Timothy 1:11). The Greek word for service, *diakonia*, can mean service of any kind.

The contrast between the pre-Christian and Christian life is sharply drawn. In his pre-Christian days Paul's vehemence escalated from words to action against the church (see Acts 9:4; 22:4; 26:9-11; 1 Corinthians 15:9; Galatians 1:13; Philippians 3:6). But still, Paul has been shown mercy (see Romans 11:30-36; 1 Corinthians 7:25; 2 Corinthians 4:1). Note that Paul does not explain his behavior away by appealing to ignorance. Paul can only depend upon the mercy and compassion of God.

Grace *superabounded* means above its usual measure (*overflowed* in the RSV).

Paul knows the love that can only come through union with Christ. For Paul, faith has replaced ignorance and unbelief. Love replaced a brutal persecution of the Christian movement. Perhaps Timothy had been questioning the power of his gospel. Perhaps it did not look like it was sufficient for the task of confronting false teachers and immoral society. The short autobiographical reference serves to underscore the immense power that is only God's. Not only does the reference underscore the apostle's authority; it also serves to undergird the flagging faith and sense of authority in Timothy. If the power of God is sufficient to overcome the intransigence of Paul, then it will be equally sufficient to stand against the false teachers' confrontation with Timothy and his church.

The saying is sure (verse 15) is the first of five such citations (the others are 1 Timothy 3:1; 4:9; 2 Timothy 2:11; Titus 3:8). The sayings are excerpts from catechetical, baptismal, or other liturgical materials. The saying echoes material from both the synoptic Gospels (see Luke 5:32) and the Gospel of John (see John 12:47).

Worthy of full acceptance can also be translated *wholehearted* or *universal.*

The reference to the incarnation implies much more than the birth of Jesus. Incarnation includes the entire ministry, life, death, and resurrection of Jesus.

Though he is now forgiven, Paul still considers himself a sinner. He refuses to stand aloof from the foibles and depths of human experience. By this time, late in his ministry, Paul was the target of many attacks ranging from criticism (see 2 Corinthians 12:10; 1 Thessalonians 2:2) to actual persecution (see Acts 13:50; 1 Corinthians 4:12). By identifying with sinful human beings, Paul subtly expresses a compassion for all persons.

In verse 16 Paul posits reasons for God's patience: (1) God's use of Paul as a living illustration of what God can do. Here *Jesus Christ* is reversed in order from earlier usage (recall 1 Timothy 1:1, 2, 12, 14, 15). This order may suggest a more personal expression with the memory of conversion fresh in his thinking (see Acts 9:5). (2) Others may then believe and (3) share in eternal life.

Having introduced a piece from liturgical usage and reflected on the work of God, Paul concludes this section with a doxology (see 1 Timothy 6:15 for a parallel). Use of doxologies is not uncommon in Paul's letters (see Romans 11:36; 16:27; Galatians 1:5; Ephesians 3:21; Philippians 4:20). This doxology could possibly be a quotation from Jewish liturgy (see Psalm 10:16). The title *King of the ages* may have been suggested by the words *eternal life.* Modern readers will see familiar words in *immortal* and *invisible,* perhaps even adding by habit the hymn's words, " . . . God only wise." The doxology closes with the traditional Hebrew expression *Amen.* Again, Paul frequently used an amen to conclude sections (see 1 Corinthians 16:24; Galatians 1:5).

Real Authority and Power (1:18-20)

The major reason for the letter, first stated in verse 5 and expanded in verse 11, is reiterated in verse 18: namely, the task of confronting false teachers. The charge to which Timothy has been assigned is not an arbitrary one. Timothy's work has no less than prophetic overtones. The ambiguous reference to prophetic utterances invites two interpretations. Perhaps Paul is alluding to prophecies that have been made about Timothy's work. Or he may be alluding to utterances that point towards the validity and authority of Timothy's ministry. These may have been expressed during Timothy's ordination. Acts 13:1-3 gives evidence that in the Christian movement prophets did have a role in the church's expansion.

The reference to *warfare* may sound offensive to the modern ear. However, the image evokes a life and death struggle between the Christian faith and the forces of evil. Paul was certainly not averse to employing powerful and graphic military imagery in describing the conflict between Christians and evil (see 1 Corinthians 9:7; 2 Corinthians 10:3; Philippians 2:25).

Holding faith and a good conscience (verse 19) suggests the intrinsic relationship between religion and morality. Recall 1:5 where religion and conscience are linked. Here Paul says in as many words that any preacher who intends to carry out the confrontation with evil must practice what he or she preaches.

Two men serve as examples of how lives can be destroyed when people reject faith and good conscience. Hymenaeus is mentioned in 2 Timothy 2:17-18. Alexander the coppersmith is mentioned in 2 Timothy 4:14, and is sometimes identified as the individual responsible for the riot stirred up in Ephesus (see Acts 19:23-29).

The expression . . . *delivered to Satan* stems from Job 2:6 where the Lord allows Satan to have his way with one of God's people. Satan, of course, is considered the primary source of both moral evil and physical disorder. The two men will be taught through stern punishment not to misrepresent God's truth. However, the punishment may not be a physical affliction. Exclusion from the church may be the intention. In 1 Corinthians 5:5 Paul instructs the church to exclude from its protective membership a man who sins openly and against the authority of the gospel.

§ § § § § § §

The Message of 1 Timothy 1

§ The Christian's hope for eternal life is through Jesus Christ.

§ Religion and ethics are not foreign to each other; they are vitally related to each other.

§ The primary purpose of Bible study is to understand and be apprehended by the salvation of God through Christ.

§ The power of God to affect salvation is sufficient even for the most angry and blasphemous individuals or circumstances.

§ The truth of Christ's work of salvation is worthy of universal acceptance.

§ Christians will always feel tension between their identity as the people of God and as members of culture and society.

§ Rejection of biblical faith can result in spiritually shipwrecked lives.

§ The Christian faith is a positive faith that leads to life and high moral standards.

§ § § § § § §

1 Timothy 2

Introduction to This Chapter

In Chapter 1 we heard the younger preacher admonished to defend the truth of the Christian gospel against false teachers. The threat to the church came from people who attempted to gain inroads into the church with their false doctrine. Chapter 2:1 begins a section which culminates in 3:15 that essentially deals with how the people of God should behave as *the household of God*. Chapter 2 addresses the need for maintaining order in public worship.

The issue of appropriate worship was not restricted to the troubled church served by Timothy. Earlier in his own ministry Paul himself had to contend with unruly factions in the Corinthian church.

Here is an outline of this chapter.

I. The Centrality of Prayer (2:1-7)

II. Spiritual Quality Versus Appearance (2:8-15)

The Centrality of Prayer (2:1-7)

Prayer is of primary importance in the Christian's public worship. Though different sorts of prayers are listed, we should not interpret this as an exhaustive or restrictive listing. Supplications are requests that stem from a deep sense of need. Prayers of a general nature are those that suggest an approach to God. The emphasis in this list seems to move towards the final two types: intercessions and thanksgiving.

Intercessory prayer is the actual petitioning of God on behalf of others. These prayers afford real power to even the most humble Christians. We must remember that the people first attracted to the movement were not the movers and shakers in society. Paul told the first Christians in the Corinthian church that *not many of you were wise according to worldly standards, not many were powerful, not many were of noble birth* (1 Corinthians 1:26). Prayer, therefore, gave to all the enormous resource of God's own power. Moreover, the congregation is to give thanks for all people. The Greek word for thanksgiving is *eucharista*, from which we receive the term for Holy Communion, the Eucharist.

The emphasis on *all men* suggests a universality that may sound peculiar at first. Why would the congregation have to be instructed to pray on behalf of all people? Scholars conclude that part of the false teaching being promulgated by the false teachers was an exclusive spirit. Exclusiveness could easily have been a Gnostic impulse since they held that only the privileged few who had a special knowledge (from the word *gnosis*) could understand truth. The exclusiveness could just as easily have been from Jewish elements, especially given the theological explanation of Jesus that follows in verses 5-7.

Perhaps Paul is concerned that the church may lose its universal message for which he had labored through missionary journey and intra-church confrontation (see Acts 15). In addition, the genius of Paul's insight is that there is no one for whom the Christian ought not pray.

To a greater or lesser extent modern readers are removed from the world in which the Pastoral Letters were first written. In order to understand verses as problematic as these (and others in the same chapter), we must attempt to reconstruct the world of first- and second-century culture and political structures.

Though history books teach of *Pax Romana*, the Roman Peace, not all textbooks include the seething anger and resentment in the populations of occupied countries. The Jews had always chafed at any occupation force. Jewish sentiment against Rome had been a major concern during the time of Jesus' ministry. A careful reading of the Passion narratives reveals that when given the choice between Barabbas and Jesus, the crowd chose to save one of their own. Why? Because Barabbas had killed a Roman soldier in an act that would have been considered foolhardy but hardly damnable.

Crucial to the continued life of the Christian movement was the maintenance of a minimally threatening, low profile stance towards the governing authorities. The Christian movement could ill afford to have both resistance from other religious interests and traditions as well as persecuting forces from the government. Therefore, in the initial years Christian interests were not primarily aimed at changing social structures. Implicit throughout the Book of Acts is the fact that the Christian movement is not meant to threaten the authority of Rome. Some scholars suggest that the Book of Acts was intended in part to offset the suspicion that the Christian movement was a subversive movement intent on toppling the emperor's authority.

For this verse, however, suffice it to say that the Christian church has been given instruction to pray for all sovereigns and others in authority. Paul gave similar counsel to the church in Rome, *Let every person be subject to the governing authorities* (Romans 13:1; see also 1 Peter 2:13-14). The notion of Christian involvement in the radical altering of societal systems is simply unthinkable in the context of the Pastoral Epistles.

The attitude of seeking the welfare of the governing authorities can also be found in the Old Testament. In Jeremiah's letter to the exiles (Jeremiah 29:1-32), the prophet counsels the exiles to *seek the welfare of the city where I have sent you into exile, and pray to the LORD on its behalf, for in its welfare you will find your welfare* (verse 7).

The results of the prayers are twofold. First, the Christian community will enjoy a quiet and peaceful life. By implication, then, the church will not have to be anxious about attack from hostile governing authority. Also, the church in Ephesus will not have to be concerned any longer about the sort of upheaval that had plagued them in the past (see Acts 19:23).

The word *respectful* (RSV) can also be translated *respectable* or *dignified*. This word picks up on Hebrew traditions of holiness and righteousness (see Luke 1:6). Only through true reverence can anyone come to know God. Here may be a subtle barb aimed at the pseudo-intellectual Gnostics who claimed to know God in a unique manner.

This is good (verse 3) refers to both the prayers themselves, that is, for all people and especially people in authority, and for the kind of life Christians lead.

Acceptable to *God our Savior* recalls 1:1.

The nature of God is that all people be saved. Here in verse 4 the writer takes on the Jewish belief that God intends the destruction of enemies and the Gnostic supposition that salvation is only for the intellectually or spiritually superior.

To come to the knowledge of the truth is a phrase found only in the Pastoral Epistles (see 2 Timothy 2:25; 3:7; Titus 1:1). A similar phrase does occur in Hebrews 10:26, though there in a different context. In the Pastorals it is a technical term that means the acceptance of or conversion to Christianity. The acceptance of Christianity means a good deal more than merely an intellectual function. The full acceptance of Christianity also means living a life commensurate with the gospel.

Verses 5-7 appear to be something of an interruption. The material could possibly be a quotation from a larger work, a catechism of some kind, or perhaps a worship liturgy. Paul interrupts himself similarly in 1 Corinthians 8:6. The theological principle of *one God* has its origins in the Old Testament. Deuteronomy 6:4-9 contains what the Hebrews call the *Shema. Hear, O Israel: The* LORD *our God is one* LORD.

The assertion that there is only *one mediator* suggests a confrontation with teachers of the Jewish tradition. No longer is Moses a mediator (see Galatians 3:19). God no longer requires a high priest (picking up on the tradition of Melchizedek in Hebrews 7:1-10, 15-16).

The mediator is not identified as divine; the divinity is assumed. The point to which Paul summons the reader is the human element. The evidence we have in the Pastorals is that the false teachers taught an ethic in which the body is considered bad. This very succinct reference is a barb against the ascetic tendencies of the heretics. This is also an allusion to the second Adam (see Romans 5:12; 1 Corinthians 15:21-22, 45-46).

Gave himself as a ransom for all (verse 6) defines the work of the mediator Jesus Christ. Paul may be alluding to the Lord's own characterization of himself in Mark 10:45.

The testimony to which was borne is ambiguous. Three possibilities can be listed. First, the testimony may have been by prophets (see Romans 3:21; 1 Peter 1:10). Second, the testimony may have been by Jesus himself (see John 18:37). Third, the witness may have been by Paul the writer (see 1 Corinthians 1:6; 2 Thessalonians 1:10).

In verse 7 Paul cites autobiographical material in order to substantiate his claim. He was appointed a herald/preacher and apostle (recall 1:1 and 12; see also Acts 9:15; 13:47; 22:21). Timothy should not be surprised that he is under attack. The writer/Paul himself still faces a stern challenge from false teachers. In the midst of it all, Paul still speaks truth (see Romans 9:1; 2 Corinthians 11:31; Galatians 1:20). Faith and truth are the topics in which Paul centers his preaching.

Two words capture the universal implications of the gospel: *all* (verse 6) and *Gentiles* (verse 7). The Christian faith has not even the first hint of exclusivity about it.

Spiritual Quality Versus Appearance (2:8-15)

In every place means in every gathering for worship, whenever the church gathers for public worship. Implicit in the gathering for worship is the preaching of the gospel. Therefore, whenever the gospel is preached, prayers will be made.

The traditional posture for prayer (Psalm 141:2) of *lifting holy hands* is linked with the attitude of the prayer. The notion of holy hands also combines the high ideal of moral purity with a sense of consecration (see 1 Peter 2:9, where the Christian is identified as one of God's chosen people, that is, *consecrated*). However, Paul refuses to allow an external posture to stand by itself. The external posture is linked with an internal or spiritual condition *without anger or quarreling* (see Matthew 6:7; 14:23; Mark 11:24-25).

In verses 9-15 the expectations of women both in worship and society receive attention. In our contemporary theological and social mood these references may be problematic at best, or highly explosive at worst. We are reading documents that were first penned in the context of ancient Roman culture, within social structures of long tradition, by individuals concerned about not only the advancement of the gospel, but also maintaining harmonious and appropriate standards of social interaction and ordering. We must not simply lift these verses, and others like them, out of their historical and sociological context as rules and regulations that apply to women of every era.

All that has been said about men is appropriate for women as well. In addition women should adorn themselves *modestly and sensibly in seemly apparel*. The word for *modestly* is found only here in the New Testament. The meaning suggests a certain propriety or inner self-governing that avoids overstepping limits of reserve or giving free release to passions. The word *sensibly* can also be translated *soberly* (see 2:15; Acts 26:25

where the word is translated *sober*). True ornamentation is not a matter of external manifestation; it has to do with what is internal.

Good deeds (verse 10) can also be translated *acts of charity*. In the Pastorals deeds of charity are not restricted only to women. Good deeds are expected of every member (see Titus 2:14; 3:8, 14). Officers should do good deeds (Titus 2:7). Members who are financially well-off are especially expected to do good deeds (1 Timothy 6:17-18). Paul expresses similar expectations in other letters as well (see Romans 2:7; 2 Corinthians 11:9; Ephesians 2:10; Colossians 1:10).

However, the motive for the good deeds is not to secure salvation. This admonition should not be interpreted to be a works-salvation motif (see 2 Timothy 2:21; Titus 3:5). Professing religion in this context means the attendance of public worship.

In verses 11-15, the letter continues with primary focus on worship. However, the inclusion of the word *submissive* suggests the larger context of relationships between husbands and wives.

In Acts 18:26 Priscilla participates in a worship service by interpreting Scriptures. Women did in fact have a place in public worship services. What Paul addresses therefore is a specific development within some of the churches under his charge. The Christian movement's new spirit of emancipation and freedom carried with it the liability of misuse. The Corinthian church certainly experienced a surge of new thinking with respect to worship (see 1 Corinthians 11:4-15). Given the evidence in the Corinthian correspondence and in First Timothy, some, presumably not all, of the women had taken their new freedom in Christ to mean they could freely express themselves in uninhibited and unguarded ways. The result seems to have been disrupted worship services.

The word *authority* here means to lord it over someone or to dictate to someone. Paul does not allow anyone, man or woman, to have authority over him. His only authority is Christ Jesus his Lord.

Verse 15 is one of the most debated verses in Scripture. Does Paul mean to suggest that a woman must have children in order to achieve salvation? Other interpretations give better insight into the nature of Paul's and Timothy's dilemma. Some of the false teachers taught a strict asceticism which included abstinence from any sexual relations. For these false teachers, salvation could come only through such public expressions as worship. To the Christian this seems incredible. Therefore, the insight is that salvation can come through the home as well, through such natural functions as childbearing.

Faith, love, and *holiness* are essential Christian virtues (see 1 Thessalonians 3:6-13).

§ § § § § § § §

The Message of 1 Timothy 2

§ Prayer is central in the Christian life.

§ Prayers are to be said for all people.

§ Prayer results in an internally tranquil life.

§ Public worship is a major part of the Christian life.

§ There is but one God, the God revealed through the Old and New Testaments, through history and the person of Jesus Christ.

§ In order for prayer to be authentic, an individual must have an attitude of prayer in addition to the posture of prayer.

§ Posture without inner attitude is sheer pretense.

§ Men and women will find salvation in part through carrying out appropriate roles in society and the home.

§ § § § § § § §

1 Timothy 3

Introduction to This Chapter

Chapter 3 presents and discusses the qualifications and character of church leadership. We will see in this chapter that Paul is very concerned that the church remain secure from criticism or censure from outsiders. Therefore, the quality of character, moral level, and intellectual qualifications for church leadership receive strong emphasis.

Here is an outline of 1 Timothy 3.

  I. Regarding Bishops (3:1-7)
 II. Regarding Deacons in the Church (3:8-10)
III. Regarding Women (3:11)
 IV. Deacons Have Greater Responsibility (3:12-13)
  V. Possible Delay in Visit (3:14-15)
 VI. An Excerpt From a Christian Hymn (3:16)

Regarding Bishops (3:1-7)

The previous chapter dealt with the decorum and ordering of public worship. Almost abruptly Paul makes a transition from the nature of public, corporate worship to the qualifications of character required in leadership.

The saying is sure (verse 1) can also be translated *faithful is the word*. Recall a similar usage in 1:15. The phrase could possibly refer to what has preceded. However, most scholars hold that it refers to what will follow. Paul may be countering a prevalent pejorative attitude toward the work of administration generally. In 1 Corinthians

12:28 Paul lists the functions to which God appoints people. Evidently administration ranked relatively low in the hierarchy of spiritual endowment. Indeed, administrators are listed only before those who speak in tongues! Another possibility is that Paul is merely citing a familiar proverb praising any who seek higher authority. Perhaps a majority of capable people avoided assuming any larger civic or ecclesiastical responsibility.

Whatever the motive behind the statement, the key word is still *good* (see also 2 Timothy 4:5). In 1 Thessalonians 5:12 Paul admonishes the Thessalonians to esteem those who labor among them and care for them in the Lord because of their work. The work of ministry in general and the demand of administrative oversight specifically are good works requiring the best possible candidates.

One further consideration is possible. Some scholars suggest that the text has been amended by a scribe. In the Greek language, very little would have to be changed to alter the text from *trustworthy is the word* to *human is the word*, picking up on common letters not immediately apparent in English translation.

Verses 2-7 describe the qualifications for a bishop, literally, an overseer. This word is the Greek *episkopos*, from which English derives *episcopal*. The term is also found in Philippians 1:1 where *bishops* and *deacons* are listed together; in Acts 20:28 where the word *overseers* is used; and in 1 Peter 2:25 where the verse reads literally, *but ye turned now to the shepherd and bishop of the souls of you*. The RSV translates, *have now returned to the Shepherd and Guardian of your souls*.

Here the word occurs in the singular. This may suggest that only one bishop works in each congregational setting. Though no duties are enumerated, we can deduce what some of the responsibilities are. The bishop presides over the public worship services of the congregation. He also exercises authority as in the family through the administration of discipline. He also teaches (verse 2), exercises control over finances (verse 3), represents the Christian community to other congregations in different areas (verse 2), and represents the Christian community to the outside world (verse 7).

The requirements for bishop are not much different from the ethical expectations demanded of all Christians. However, some of the requirements are distinctly for the unique position of episcopal leadership. Compare this list with Titus 1:5-9, where a similar list of requirements has the tone of systematized or stereotyped organization. Scholars have pointed out that the list of requirements is roughly similar to what is expected of a Stoic wise man (that is, a married man, not puffed up, and one temperate with wine).

The list contains two sets of requirements. The first has to do with how the bishop lives life generally within his family (one wife, temperate, sensible, orderly) and within the community (not an excessive drinker, not a striker of people, forbearing, and not quarrelsome). The second applies specifically to the service of his duties (hospitable and an apt teacher).

The bishop must be *above reproach* (see also 5:7; 6:14; and Titus 1:6), especially in the realm of sexual behavior. Paul wants to protect the church from any criticism or censure, possible if the higher and public authority fails at any of these requirements.

The first requirement, *the husband of one wife,* has evoked great debate. The phrase can be interpreted in many ways. To begin with, we can be quite certain that it prohibits polygamy (more than one wife at a time). The bishop is certainly to exercise fidelity in his own marriage and should not have either a concubine or a mistress. However, does the writer mean to contend that the bishop must be a married man? Given the context of the rest of the requirements with the heavy emphasis on the family, we may conclude so. Among the false teachings challenging the congregation are some that deprecate marriage (see 4:3 where some forbid marriage altogether). Any admonition that the bishop must be married goes against the implication of Matthew 19:12 and Paul's personal assertion in 1 Corinthians 7:8-9.

Another possibility concerns the practice of divorce. Does the writer mean to suggest that a bishop should not divorce his present wife and remarry? Or does the writer mean to contend that if a man aspiring to the office of bishop has been married but has suffered the loss of his wife to death he should not remarry? These possibilities enliven the discussion and shed light on the complexities confronting the original audience as well as modern commentators and teachers.

Temperate can also be translated *clearheaded*. The term is found only here and in Titus 2:2. For a similar notion see 1 Peter 1:13 where the term *sober* is used. The term originally referred to avoiding drunkenness (see 1 Thessalonians 5:6, 8 where Paul makes assertions about drunkenness). Paul may well intend a broader application for the Ephesian congregation in which Timothy labors.

Sensible may also be translated *self-controlled, prudent,* or *orderly.* The implication here is that the bishop will not only exhibit external orderly personal and administrative skills, but that he will have an internal order, a spiritual life that undergirds and makes external ordering possible.

The teaching ministry of the church came under episcopal authority and leadership. Not only would the bishop be a skilled teacher in the technical sense. He would also adhere to the tradition of apostolic teaching and doctrine. Implied through the Pastoral Letters is the tacit understanding that the bishop (indeed all leaders) would be prepared to confront any false teaching (see Titus 1:9).

Evidently some church leaders had taken their authority regarding discipline to the point of physical abuse. A bishop should not abuse any church member. In sharp contrast to the violent tendencies of some, the bishop is to be *gentle*, that is, magnanimous, with gracious condescension and forbearing. Could this be an allusion to Paul's earlier assertion that he would be all things to all people that some should be saved?

Since the bishop will have primary concern for the church's finances, he should not be overly concerned about amassing fortune nor should he be attached to money. This same concern is voiced in Titus 1:7.

In verses 4-5 Paul illustrates the bishop's authority through the example of the family. If the bishop is to manage his administration well, he must be able to handle his family life with wisdom.

The term *God's church* is found only twice in the New Testament: here and in verse 15. In the Greek no definite article occurs. The implication therefore, is for any church, not just a specific church. The notion of exclusivity in claim on truth or denominational impulse is alien to the first- and second-century Christian movement.

Perhaps Paul reflects in verse 6 on his own experience of a fourteen-year hiatus following his dramatic conversion. Any man who aspires to high office should not be a recent convert. This may refer solely to the event of conversion. In addition, the reference could easily imply that a bishop should not have been recently baptized. In 1 Corinthians 3:6 Paul uses the term *planted*, which implies beginnings of Christian growth in people. Perhaps he has some of those individuals in mind.

Puffed up with conceit can also be translated *swollen-headed*. In the Greek the image is also of a person enshrouded in smoke, thus indicating a clouding of judgment. The term is intended to evoke images both of deceit and of folly, yielding arrogant behavior and erroneous teaching. However, poor judgment is not the only liability of swollen-headedness.

Not surprisingly, Paul reiterates the goal in verse 7 that any Christian, especially one aspiring to high office, should not embarrass or otherwise bring reproach from outsiders. If a minister acts in a way contrary to these admonitions, he may bring criticism not only on himself as an individual but also on the entire church as well.

Regarding Deacons in the Church (3:8-10)

As in Philippians 1:1 the deacons are linked with bishops. Though functions are not enumerated, they must have been similar. The deacons' work may have included assistance in worship services as well as acts of charity and good deeds on behalf of the poorer members of the congregation.

The qualifications for the office parallel those of a bishop. To begin with, deacons must be of a serious nature both with respect to their spiritual lives as well as their outward appearance. They must not be double-tongued or tale-bearers as they make their rounds from house to house. The word for *double-tongued* occurs only here in the New Testament.

They should not be heavy drinkers nor should they be avaricious. Both expectations parallel the expectations listed in verse 3.

The *mystery of the faith* (verse 9) may be translated *the secret truths of the Christian faith*. More precisely, without possible allusion to the mystery religions surrounding the Christian movement, the phrase refers to the understanding of true religion and true morality. In 1 Corinthians 2:7 Paul refers to the Christian faith as *a secret and hidden wisdom of God*. The notion of mystery occurs many times in Paul's writing. (See 1 Corinthians 4:1; 13:2; 14:2; 15:51; Colossians 1:26; 2:2; 4:3.) The word carries within it the open secret of the history of salvation preached by the church. In the context of 1 Timothy there is an element of correctness in its doctrine as well (see the creed/hymnal fragment that follows in verse 16).

According to verse 10 the testing does not necessarily mean a formal period of examination. More probably it means a general evaluation of the individual's character, conduct, and qualifications for the position.

Regarding Women (3:11)

No identification is given as to who these women are. Since they are placed directly following discussion of the deacons, they may well be women who perform tasks of service within the church, thus suggesting a designation of deaconesses. Paul speaks of Phoebe's work using the term *deaconess* in Romans 16:1. However, the office of deaconess did not develop until the fourth century. Some commentators suggest that the women are the deacons' wives. In any event, the women are to exhibit the same characteristics that are demanded of the male deacons: They must be serious-minded, not slanderers or gossipers, and temperate.

Deacons Have Greater Responsibility (3:12-13)

Abruptly in verse 12 Paul resumes the charge to deacons through reference to marriage and family. Does this mean that the deacons had to be married as a part of their qualifications? The implication seems to be that deacons will aspire to the higher office of bishop, and therefore must fulfill the external requirements of marriage and family.

The deacons' exemplary behavior will yield a moral advantage of an increased authority and therefore a larger influence in the community. Clearly the aim is not merely for personal advancement. The exemplary behavior is greater confidence in their faith in Christ Jesus.

Possible Delay in Visit (3:14-15)

Paul intends to visit with Timothy and the congregation presumably to strengthen both Timothy's resolve as well as his authority in the congregation. However, circumstances may prevent the visit. These instructions refer at least to Chapters 1 and 2, if not the entire letter.

Again, Paul draws attention to true character, the knowledge of the truth (a recurrent theme through the Pastorals), and household of God.

The Greek word here translated *church* is *ecclesia*.

Reference to the *living God* may be a response to the presence of heathen gods in the surrounding culture. Moreover, the notion of a living God suggests a vital, vibrant power that makes the moral life possible (see also 4:10; 6:13).

The metaphor of pillars is somewhat difficult to understand. Perhaps Paul has in mind a large building in which many pillars work cooperatively to support the structure. The implication then is that individual Christians live in community and can thus be reinforced as they live out exemplary moral lives. The word *pillar* is used elsewhere to describe individuals (see Galatians 2:9 and Revelation 3:12).

An Excerpt From a Christian Hymn (3:16)

The introduction to this hymn fragment is similar to other introductions of doctrinal formulas (recall 1:15; 2:3-5).

The hymn is introduced by a type of confessional formula, *by common agreement,* that is, *we confess* (RSV). The saying, *Great . . . is the mystery* also sounds like a formulaic saying similar to the assertion in Ephesus found in Acts 19:28, 34.

The fragment consists of two stanzas of three lines each. The first stanza emphasizes the life of Jesus as incarnate Lord. The second stanza emphasizes the life of the ascended Lord.

The mystery of our religion, that is, the revealed secret of true religion, is the person Jesus Christ (see Colossians 1:27). Religion included doctrinal formulations as well as the moral life. In the Pastoral Epistles both are of great concern.

The structure of the hymn is as follows.

The Life Incarnate
  —as seen on earth *(manifested in the flesh)*
  —as observed from heaven *(seen by angels)*
The Life of the Ascended Lord
  —as preached *(preached among the nations)*
  —as lived in heaven *(taken up in glory)*

The word for *manifestation* is *epiphania*, from which the Christian church takes the term *Epiphany*. In the Christian liturgical calendar the Epiphany is marked with the narratives of the wise men from the east visiting the newborn babe. The manifestation/Incarnation means much more than the birth. The term includes the entire life, ministry, death, and resurrection of Jesus.

In the flesh emphasizes the humanity of Jesus. Some of the false teachers attempted to deprecate the importance of humanity by denying Jesus' humanity. The Christian church immediately recognized the danger in such theology.

The phrase *vindicated by the Spirit* is very difficult to interpret. The saying is set in the context of contrasts between spirit and flesh, world and glory, heavenly powers and nations. Therefore, it may refer to the entrance of Jesus into the divine realm through his triumph over the world. It may also be an affirmation of Jesus' claims in Matthew 12:28, *If it is by the Spirit of God that I cast out demons, then the kingdom of God has come upon you.* See also Romans 1:3-4 and Colossians 2:15.

Angels watching Jesus refers to two factors. The allusion is first to the angels that attended him in his earthly life (see Mark 1:13; Luke 2:13) and then to those who watched his resurrection (see Luke 24:23).

This same Jesus is preached among the nations. Note the allusion to the universality of Jesus and the gospel. The term *nations* is deliberately ambiguous. Nations can mean humankind generally or Gentiles in particular. According to the Gospel tradition (Matthew 24:14; 28:19; Mark 13:10), the gospel must be preached in order for history to come to its consummation. The universality of the gospel is meant by *in the world*.

The final phrase deals with the Ascension (see Acts 1:2, 11, 22). Christ is accepted not only throughout the world, the *cosmos*, but in the heavenly places as well. In the heavenly realm he lives in glory and communicates his glory to humankind.

§ § § § § § §

The Message of 1 Timothy 3

In this chapter we have seen Paul describe high moral standards of life to which church leadership should aspire. His concern is that the church remain free from criticism or censure by scoffing outsiders. What else can we learn from this chapter?

§ Administrative work should be understood as legitimate ministry.

§ Leaders must exhibit concern and not coercion over their charge.

§ True character is both an external manifestation and an internal state.

§ Ministries of menial tasks are valid, as well as the more highly visible tasks and those of respected greater authorities.

§ We may not be prepared to call the force of evil the devil, but we can be certain that evil forces do set traps and await our entrapment.

§ We need each other in the church to help reinforce our higher calling.

§ The humanity of Jesus is as much a blessing as is the divinity of Jesus.

§ § § § § § §

1 Timothy 4

Introduction to This Chapter

In the first few verses of the letter Paul alludes to false teachers. Now he will address the threat that the false teachers pose to individuals and to the church as a whole. The major areas of false teaching included (1) prohibition of marriage, (2) prohibition of certain foods, and (3) an unguarded enthusiasm and distortion of the resurrection.

Here is an outline of 1 Timothy 4.

I. A Warning Against False Teaching (4:1-5)
II. Words to Timothy About His Teaching (4:6-11)
III. About His Gifts and Authority (4:12-16)

A Warning Against False Teaching (4:1-5)

The Spirit finds expression through human agents such as prophets. But the Spirit also expresses itself through Paul. Not only did Jesus anticipate the emergence of false teachers, and Paul predict false teachers as wolves within the church of God, but the Spirit too had forewarned through prophets. Acts 11:27-30 contains the narrative of a prophet who forewarned a famine through the Spirit.

Paul begins with an allusion to the Spirit, the strongest possible declaration of authority for what he is about to argue (see Acts 20:23; 21:11).

The phrase *later times* probably refers to some future time. The term also implies the indefinite period before the day of the Lord (see Matthew 24:2-6; 1 John 2:18).

The events and stresses that Paul sees in Ephesus give evidence that the later crisis is in fact occurring at the present moment (see 1 John 4:1-3).

The threat of deceitful spirits is addressed in a number of New Testament documents. First John 4:6 speaks of the contradiction between the *spirit of truth* and the *spirit of error*. Paul's letter to Corinth (1 Corinthians 10:20-21) contains the word *demons* to describe false gods to whom sacrifices had been offered by pagans. James 3:15 speaks of demon-like wisdom. Revelation 16:14 includes a reference to demonic spirits. Clearly the writer and the congregation believed in the power of evil taking on demonic forms. In the New Testament mind, the power of evil is personified.

Names of people are not given, but their characteristics are listed in verse 2. The demonic people are pretentious, liars, and can no longer distinguish between right and wrong (see Ephesians 4:19). *Liars* in this context suggests much more than merely not telling the truth. These people are also hypocrites of the first order since they have no consistency between what they preach and what they practice (see Romans 2:17-23).

The identification of branding (the RSV has *seared*) takes its cue from the practice of branding slaves on the forehead for identification purposes.

The actual content of the false teachers' teaching is given in verse 3. It includes ascetic practices of abstinence from both marriage and certain foods. In Gnostic teaching marriage was often forbidden, especially in the second century. The Essene sect (Qumran community near the Dead Sea, known to us primarily for its scrolls) spoke against marriage. Here Paul does not attempt a corrective. He has already done that by speaking to the marriage status of aspiring bishops and deacons. Furthermore, Paul affirms marriage by blessing the role of women in childbearing (2:15; 5:14). In Titus 2:4 Paul admonishes young women to love their husbands.

With respect to food the false teachers were equally demanding. Evidently the heretics were against alcohol (see 5:23). From the concern about certain foods, scholars conclude that at least one element of the false teachers was of strong Jewish traditional rootage. Titus 1:10-11 addresses issues primarily related to Jewish ritual food regulations. Paul had to contend with similar issues in other churches as well (see Romans 14:14, 23; 1 Corinthians 8:7).

Why is Paul disturbed about the false teaching? Had he not earlier admonished the Corinthians not to make too much of specific individual scruples with respect to food? He sees clearly the inherent danger of people confusing obedience to certain regulations with the substance of working out salvation. Salvation by works is always a peril in the religious community.

Moreover, the false teachers seem to speak with a self-assurance that exceeds a proper humility. In 2 Timothy 2:18 the false teachers seem unconcerned that their teaching is upsetting the faith of others. Teachers or preachers should speak with an appropriate stutter when they say more than they know.

All food is to be received with thanksgiving. In Romans 14:6 Paul charges Christians to eat *in honor of the Lord* and giving *thanks to God*. In his letter to Corinth (1 Corinthians 10:30) Paul reflects on his own thanksgiving when he eats. To the Philippians (4:6) Paul expands the notion from eating to giving thanks for all things.

Those who believe refers to Christians who have accepted the gospel and know the truth.

The truth means the Christian gospel (recall 2:4).

In verse 4 Paul interprets the issue in a larger theological context. The primary theological principle that undergirds Paul's thinking is the creative work of God in Genesis 1. In this account, when God completes each segment of creation, God pronounces that creation to be good. No exceptions are made.

Receiving food with thanksgiving here means a grace of some sort before meals. Where the Gospels portray Jesus taking food, they always show Jesus giving thanks (see Mark 6:41; 8:6; 14:22; Luke 24:30).

The term *consecrated* (verse 5) may cause difficulty in interpretation. The prayer itself does not make the formerly unclean food clean. The prayer of thanks alters the receiver's thinking and perspective. Grace puts food in its appropriate perspective. Food is a gift from God, from the fertile earth of God's creation.

Words to Timothy About His Teaching (4:6-11)

The verb used in this instruction is not one of heavy authority. Instead, the younger preacher is told *If you put . . . .* Perhaps the milder word is used with deliberate thought given to the relative age of Timothy. The younger man would hardly be in a good position to make demands on his older colleagues. Another translation could possibly be *supply to the brothers,* which would pick up on the metaphor of building in 3:15.

Brothers continues the metaphor of family/household of God (recall 3:15). Later, in 5:1, further advice is given that Timothy should treat older men as fathers, younger men like brothers. (See also 6:1.)

The instructions, or suggestions (in keeping with the gentler verb), refer to the principles that have already been summarized in verses 1-5, though they could also refer to the entire previous section of the letter as well.

The word used for *minister* is *diakonia* (deacon). The function of the minister seems to have become more specialized. Various translations add depth and shadow to the understanding of the word; admirable minister, true servant, or excellent minister.

How is any minister to attain the high goal of good or admirable? Paul continues by using the image of feeding and nourishment. In 1 Corinthians 3:2 Paul uses the image of feeding when he summarizes his early work with the Corinthian congregation. Ministry in any setting, but especially in circumstances of conflict, stress, and questioned authority, requires the minister to maintain the disciplines of faith and good doctrine.

Faith, as we have seen (recall 4:3), means the entire Christian faith as something received/accepted. Doctrine includes the various systematized understandings, confessions, affirmations, and creeds that a true believer will learn. Evidently Timothy has kept these disciplines in the past. However, he cannot let the disciplines lapse.

In direct contrast to the necessary, healthy disciplines of the Christian life, Paul lists practices of the false teachers. The term translated as *godless and silly myths* can also be translated in a much more expressive phrase capturing a tone of condescension, *old wives' tales.* Silly myths have been mentioned earlier (recall 1:4).

Using a metaphor from the realm of athletic effort, Paul further underscores the necessity of maintaining diligent personal habits in the spiritual life. Explosive and vibrant metaphors help to capture the urgency and life-experience of his idea. In his letter to the Corinthians Paul uses a similar image (see 1 Corinthians 9:24-27).

Since Paul continues by suggesting that physical training is of some value (verse 8), we may infer that at least part of the false teaching stresses physical discipline to an extreme. Physical discipline is a legitimate part of the Christian life. In 1 Corinthians 7:25-40 Paul recommends abstinence from sexual activity as a part of the Christian life. However, the counsel to Timothy counters any ascetic implications or assertions. Apparently physical or ascetic discipline had become ends in themselves rather than means to an end.

The saying is sure and worthy of full acceptance (verse 9) sounds like another formula introduction. Recall that a similar formula was used in 1:15. The introduction probably refers to the preceding verse. Note the reiteration of the universal implications of the gospel. The saying is worth all peoples' effort and attention.

What is the goal toward which Christians *toil and strive* (Colossians 1:29)? Verse 8 has already stated the hope of the coming eternal life. *Struggle/strive* here in verse 10 does not intimate persecution as in Hebrews 10:32-33; 13:13; 1 Peter 4:14-16.

The Christian hope (1 Corinthians 15:19; 2 Corinthians 1:10) is set on the *living* God who alone is able to give life (recall the implication of 3:15). Not only is God the living God, but God is *the Savior of all* people, *especially those who believe*. The assertion that God saves all people may trouble some modern Christian readers. The original letter carries within it the suggestion that only from the living God comes life. In this sense, only God can save all people just as only God can give life. Similarly, only God can protect people from the danger of evil or demonic forces at large in the cosmos. Furthermore, only God can stir the deeper impulse to feel the desire to know God.

By placing *especially those who believe* directly following the assertion of God's character of universal Savior, Paul illustrates the necessity of individuals' appropriation of God's salvation through belief. In short, the difference between individuals is not God's design or intention. The difference in people depends upon their willingness to believe. The choice is not God's, for God would choose salvation for all. The burden of choice rests with individuals.

Previously, Paul used the verb *place* or *suggest* (verse 6). Here a much stronger verb is used. *Command* carries with it the connotation of greater authority. The word *command* does not appear in the letter to Titus (compare with Titus 2:15 where Titus is instructed to *declare* these things.).

About His Gifts and Authority (4:12-16)

The subject of Timothy's age is brought up. Evidently the congregation is made up of people who are older than Timothy and who have either disregarded Timothy's preaching and teaching outright or scoffed at his relatively young age. A young man at this time would have been one of military age, or from his twenties through roughly forty years old. Timothy may well have been in his thirties.

Timothy is not to challenge the older generation to debate or arbitrary exercise of authority. Instead, the younger minister should set an example of what the faithful individual really looks like in life and practice. To the Philippian congregation Paul had issued a similar invitation (Philippians 3:17). To the Thessalonians Paul defended himself (2 Thessalonians 3:9).

Timothy's example is to be exercised in five aspects of everyday life:
(1) in conversation with all believers,
(2) in general conduct and demeanor with grace as a characteristic attribute,
(3) in love in the Christian sense,
(4) in faith in the sense of being faithful or an individual of fidelity,
(5) in purity, meaning more than strict adherence to a high sexual ethic. Purity here means an overall attitude and behavior.

In verse 13 Paul suggests an ethic for the meantime. Timothy, like all Christians, must live in the meanwhile, between the promised visit, from the older apostle; between the presence of Jesus on earth and the promised return of the exalted Christ. Perhaps Timothy and the congregation had developed a certain lethargy with respect to the regular routine of Christian community living. Here Timothy must work diligently at the tasks of ministry in the church: Scripture reading, exhortation, and teaching.

The Scriptures of the church at this time would have been the Old Testament (see the Introduction). Scripture reading was a vital element in the Jewish synagogue tradition. Recall Luke's narrative of Jesus' return to

Nazareth (Luke 4:16-30). In Acts 15:21 the reading of the Torah is mentioned. Paul refers to the reading of the *old covenant*, that is the Old Testament, in worship services (2 Corinthians 3:14).

In this context these specific instructions do not mean a simple suggestion to read the Bible regularly. Instead, Paul is maintaining the authority of the Scriptures in Christian public worship. In addition to the Old Testament, some letters of the apostles would occasionally be read. In 1 Thessalonians 5:27 Paul gives specific instructions that *this letter be read to all the brethren*. To the Colossian church similar instructions are given. Revelation 1:3 mentions the reading of apocalypses in worship.

Exhortation includes both exposition of the texts and application of them to life. Acts 13:15 illustrates the pattern of worship that gave Paul the opportunity to preach.

The teaching ministry included instruction of new members in catechism (see Romans 12:7 where teaching is listed as a task of ministry).

In a very gracious manner Paul hints at what may be one of Timothy's primary problems (verse 14). He may have backed away from the disciplines that inform and sustain a ministry. Perhaps Timothy has neglected the disciplines that are needed to keep the special spirit that has been his from the outset. Special gifts are bestowed by the Holy Spirit (see Romans 12:6-8). In addition to the public work of ministry and reading of Scriptures, Timothy is to attend to his own study and reading of Scriptures.

Paul reminds Timothy of the high moment of his ordination when the council laid hands on his head. The gift is not understood and received by Timothy only. The Christian community also verifies and authorizes the exercise of that gift.

The laying on of hands accompanies many actions of gift giving and receiving. Jesus blesses the children by laying his hands upon them (Mark 10:16). Jesus healed with the touch of his hand (Mark 6:5). The Holy Spirit is given to the newly-baptized through the laying on of hands in Acts 8:17; 19:6. Work of both great and lesser magnitude is initiated through the laying on of hands. In Acts 6:6 the choice of servers is validated through prayer and laying on of hands. Paul is sent off on a missionary journey after the laying on of hands (Acts 13:3).

Since he leads the public worship services, Timothy's study and reading also imply a careful selection of Scriptures to be read in worship. There may be a suggestion as well that Timothy practice the oral reading of the Scriptures so as to be more effective in the reading for public hearing. Earlier Paul has spoken of the essential integrity of internal and external disciplines and actions as they are negatively manifested in the false teachers. Here he admonishes the younger preacher to see to it that he practices diligently his own personal spiritual disciplines.

In verse 16 Paul may be reflecting on a moment in his own ministry when he found himself prey to the temptation to think of himself as different from those to whom he preached and with whom he ministered.

In Paul's estimation the excellence to which Timothy is called is hardly a coincidence with what he maintains in his personal spiritual life. Timothy must keep an eye on his discipline; he must be internally motivated and self-monitoring. However, Timothy's discipline is not merely a matter of self-serving interest. The goal is not only personal salvation, but includes the salvation of all. An exclusivist attitude regarding salvation is simply not a fully Christian impulse.

§ § § § § § §

The Message of 1 Timothy 4

The younger preacher finds himself challenged by false teachers. The admonitions of the older apostle imply the image of a timid young minister taken aback by the antagonists in the congregation. What will be the best means by which to undo the potential harm of the false teachers? Public confrontation is not recommended. Instead, Paul points toward the power of personal moral influence in a world that can comprehend only coercion.

True authority is that which emerges from the confluence of personal identity (that is, Timothy's identity as Christian, minister, preacher, and teacher) with the power of God (gained through personal disciplines of study, prayer, and cultivation of spiritual life). Timothy is not instructed to challenge in debate. Nor is he told to humiliate the opponents. What else can we learn from this chapter?

§ The power of God can overcome the power of evil.

§ Absolute abstinence is not necessarily a Christian response to life.

§ Life's attitudes and actions are not simply coincidental.

§ The source of the highest attitudes and actions is faith.

§ The spiritual life requires discipline just as athletic endeavor requires physical discipline.

§ Physical disciplines have their place for the Christian, but not as ends in themselves.

§ The strongest authority a Christian has is in the authority of personal life and moral example.

§ Scriptures must remain a central part of both public worship and private devotional life.

§ § § § § § §

PART FIVE

1 Timothy 5

Introduction to This Chapter

Here is an outline of Chapter 5, which is concerned with counsel regarding different classes.

I. Older Men and Younger Men (5:1)
II. Older Women (5:2)
III. Widows (5:3-16)
IV. Presbyters (5:17-25)

Older Men and Younger Men (5:1)

In the Greek language the term for *older man* is *presbyter*. The same word is used to describe an official position and function. In this context, however, the term means an older man. This admonition is rooted in the Old Testament law of Leviticus 19:32.

Following earlier counsel (3:3), Paul reiterates the Christian pastor's responsibility not to treat anyone roughly. Furthermore, the younger preacher is not to rebuke the older men. The suggestion in essence is that if the younger preacher feels the necessity to correct another man, he should do so with careful consideration given to his age.

Some scholars interpret the word *father* here to mean that Timothy actually addressed the older men as father (and older women as mother). But this cannot be proven beyond doubt. The point is that the younger preacher is to afford great respect and honor to the older members of his congregation.

Older Women (5:2)

Regarding the women of the congregation Paul seems to suggest two pieces of advice. First, the older women are to be afforded the same respect as his mother. In Romans Paul refers to another older woman as his mother (Romans 16:13). With regard to the younger women Paul seems to be drawing on his experience and observation of ministry. The younger women are to be treated as *sisters* with the further condition of *all purity*.

Widows (5:3-16)

After rather general and cursory instructions, there follows a detailed listing regarding care for the widows in the church. The care for widows is not distinctively Christian. Deeply embedded in the Old Testament is an ongoing concern for the widows of the nation. In part this may stem from a universal concern for the suffering endured by the truly destitute and alone. (See Deuteronomy 10:18; 24:17; Isaiah 1:17; Luke 2:37.)

Apparently, some of the widows misused or abused their role (see verses 12 and 13). The difficulty caused by widows must have been particularly demanding, since this list includes instructions that exceed the length of instructions regarding both bishops and deacons.

One other possibility remains. The instructions could possibly be addressed to two different classes of widows. Verses 4-8 imply widows that are dealt with according to need. Verses 9-15 suggest a class that performs acts of charity (*good deeds* in the RSV; see verse 10).

The designation *real widow* is applied to women who have no family or friends from whom they can exact support. Interpreting from silence, since the texts give no specific reason for restricting the scope of the church's ministry, is tentative. In all likelihood the motive is careful monitoring and stewardship of the church's limited resources.

The word translated *religious duty* (RSV) can also be

translated *true piety*, a term often used to describe loyalty to the emperor (recall Paul's concern for maintenance of loyalty to the established government in 2:2).

True religion is learned first in the home, where both doctrine and action are stressed. The lessons learned include: respect for parents, reverence for all of God's family (see 3:15), and reverence for God. True religion learned in the family will be acted out through caring and supporting the older members.

Apparently some widows either stretched the definition of widowhood or abused it outright. Paul gives a rather extended definition of what a widow is. She is one who has no one to support her. She is alone in the world and has no hope whatever except for the community and care of the church. A true widow is one who has only the hope of prayer and God's continued presence to sustain her in an otherwise hostile world. Luke 2:37 gives a succinct summary of just such a widow, Anna, who worshiped, fasted, and prayed night and day. There may have been a set of prescribed prayers to be said at evening and early morning.

In sharp contrast to the worthy widow is the woman who, though not married, lives a life of wanton luxury and misses some of the power of the word (see James 5:5). This kind of individual is already living what Revelation 3:1 calls a life of death. A woman who lives a profligate life has absolutely no claim on the church's meager resources. Paul's concern for the reputation of the Christian community is once again voiced.

In verse 8 Paul resumes the argument from verse 4 regarding responsibilities. However, here the prescription is narrowed to family responsibilities. Earlier (4:10) the scope had been universal. (See also Galatians 6:10.)

Using very strong language Paul contends that lack of Christian charity shows absence of faith. Indeed, anyone who speaks of faith without an attendant action of charity is worse than a nonbeliever.

Following a long description of worthy and unworthy recipients, Paul gives specific instructions regarding widows in verse 9. A list or roster is to be assembled. In order to be placed on this list a woman must be over sixty, presumably the age when sexual impulses and desire for marriage have ceased. The age of sixty was also considered the time of retirement.

The expression *having been the wife of one husband* has been interpreted in many ways. Previously Paul has already enumerated the requirements for bishops and deacons (3:2, 12). In verse 14 Paul does recommend that younger widows remarry. Is he presenting an impossible paradox? No, he knows full well the power of passions. He presents the ideal of maintaining one marriage characterized by fidelity. Recall that among the strongest desires Paul has for the Christian church is a high ideal that is both beyond reproach and absolutely removed from scandal.

According to verse 10, widows performed a certain set of functions in the church. These women probably not only reared their own children but cared for orphans as well. Their duties also included extending hospitality to travelers. In Acts 16:14-15 Paul encounters Lydia, a merchant, who is baptized. Following her baptism she entertains the apostle in her home. In all likelihood Phoebe, mentioned in Romans 16:1, offered similar hospitality to traveling missionaries.

The practice of washing the feet of saints is rooted in the Old Testament. In 1 Samuel 25:40-42 David's intended wife Abigail washes the feet of David's servants. Luke reports the dramatic incident of the woman washing Jesus' feet while he sat at table in a Pharisee's home (Luke 7:36-38). Jesus himself washes the disciples' feet in the upper room (John 13:3-20).

Following the list of reaponsibilities performed by widows, Paul gives a brief explanation for the restrictions in verses 11-13. First, younger women who take the vow of widowhood may grow restless with the limitations. Their restlessness may lead to inappropriate behavior that violates their vows. In Greek the word for *vow* or *pledge* is *faith*. The many-faceted word carries with it strong connotations linking vow and Christian faith.

Evidently the younger widows have time on their hands in which they can only learn to be idlers. Interestingly, the term *learn* is one usually used to described a man's learning of a profession. Paul employs irony to prove his point. All that can result from such learning is flitting from house to house carrying little more than gossip and saying things they should not say. In Acts 19:19 the same word for busybodies is used to describe the magical arts of would-be exorcists.

Paul's concern in verse 15 is no casual musing on possible developments. Potential threat has turned into actual event for certain people who have been turned aside from the faith to follow false teachers (see Acts 20:30) or violate their vow to widowhood, or by living lives as described in verse 13. To Paul the threat is a dual threat of internal lack of faith and external criticism.

Verse 16 seems somewhat misplaced. Could it not easily follow the principles of verse 4 or verse 8? Financial burdens for the church are not a new invention. From the very beginning the Christian church has had to wrestle with demands that exceed immediate resources. In his second letter to the Corinthian church Paul explains his actions with regard to the potential burden he would cause for the church (2 Corinthians 11:9; 12:16). In another letter Paul recalls for the Thessalonians his refusal to burden the already stretched economics of the church (1 Thessalonians 2:9; 2 Thessalonians 3:8).

Why does Paul designate a woman in the church? First, some scholars contend that some manuscripts contain the words *man or woman* or simply *man*. However, if Paul does address one woman she is probably a woman of substantial wealth who really can help the church.

Presbyters (5:17-25)

An abrupt shift brings Paul to consider elders, here mentioned for the first time in the Pastoral Epistles. The term used for *elder* is *presbyter*. The term is ambiguous since it is used as a description for an older man as well as for a specific function within the church. (See Acts 11:30; 14:23; James 5:14.) In this verse the term means a figure in the church, since *double honor*, a form of remuneration, is to be given to him.

Paul uses the word *labor* to describe ministry (see Romans 16:12; 1 Corinthians 15:10; Galatians 4:11; Philippians 2:16). The men who exercise administrative leadership should receive more honor, or payment.

Paul does not exercise authority arbitrarily. As in other instances (see Romans 4:3; 9:17; 11:2-3; Galatians 4:30) he underscores his instructions with scriptural authority, here citing Deuteronomy 25:4. In 1 Corinthians 9:9-14 he had used the same text. The reference may also be to Matthew 10:10, where Jesus argues that a worker (that is, a preacher) is entitled to an appropriate payment.

All executive leadership is not immune to the foibles and weaknesses afflicting the rest of the church (verses 19-20). Occasionally charges are brought against them. In keeping with Jewish tradition, more than a single witness is required (see Deuteronomy 19:15; Matthew 18:16; John 8:17).

In verse 21 Paul may have a specific individual in mind with whom the congregation is familiar. The already intimidating threat is further underscored through the rapid allusion to God, Christ Jesus, and angels. The image of final judgment is thus suggested. These figures are those who will in fact take part in the final judgment (see Matthew 25:3 where the *Son of man* and the *angels* will take part; Mark 8:38 links the *Son of man*, the *Father*, and the *holy angels*). The implied meaning is quite clear. The elders have been appointed to positions of authority from which, presumably, they will exercise judgment over subordinates. But their position should not be construed in any sense to suggest that they themselves will not be similarly judged.

The elect angels are chosen by God as God's ministers. In 1 Corinthians 11:10 Paul considers angels as administering the divine order. (See also Hebrews 1:14; Revelation 14:10.)

In order to preclude a number of potential problems Paul recommends a deliberate delay in ordination (verse 22). In the flush of enthusiasm following conversion, some individuals wanted to become immediately involved in ministry. However, Paul wants to monitor the character and work of each minister.

Verse 23 is a personal digression. The expression *drink only water* is found only here in the New Testament. Perhaps Timothy had, in reaction to the charges of the false teachers, become a teetotaler. By doing so he may have adversely affected his health. Paul's argument, then, is that a discipline that harms the individual is of little worth.

In verses 24-25 the letter returns to the theme of elders and prospective leaders. Elders should be able to discern the mistakes as well as the praiseworthy efforts of younger ordinands. But even if they are not able to see everything, what is now secret will eventually become apparent. The converse is equally as true—what is good now may not be readily apparent but will become public at a later time. All of life's good and evil will be known at the final judgment. Note that Paul does not restrict his considerations to a faultfinding criticism by elders. Careful examination should be done in order to ascertain what is praiseworthy and what is unacceptable.

§ § § § § § §

The Message of 1 Timothy 5

First Timothy reveals an imperfect church trying its best to live an authentic witness surrounded by a pagan and sometimes hostile culture. Demands are made on the limited resources of the church by needy people. However, other not-so-needy people make their demands as well. Preachers and would-be preachers are subject to charges of misconduct. Paul responds to the very real demand of a real church.

What else can we learn from this chapter?

§ All individuals in the church should be given a measure of respect.

§ Christian beliefs and attitudes toward others are learned first in the home.

§ Even the most destitute are cared for by God.

§ Self-indulgent lives are more a living death than the abundant life God intends for every person.

§ Extending hospitality to other Christians is an essential good work to be done by all Christians.

§ The church is always under scrutiny by a sometimes hostile surrounding culture.

§ Preachers and preachers who teach are entitled to an appropriate payment for their ministry.

§ Scriptures are part of the authority to which all Christians should submit their thinking and instruction.

§ Ministers will be wise not to practice favoritism.

§ Religious disciplines should not harm individuals' health.

§ Good deeds may not be immediately apparent, but they will be known by God.

§ Evil deeds may remain hidden for the moment, but they will eventually be known to God.

§ § § § § § §

PART SIX

1 Timothy 6

Introduction to This Chapter

Chapter 6 begins with a discussion concerning slaves. The balance of Chapter 6, verses 3-21, picks up the argument that had begun the letter, namely, the false teachers. In the earlier chapter however, the emphasis had been on the content of the teaching itself. In this final chapter the emphasis is on the character of the teachers themselves.

Here is an outline of Chapter 6.
  I. Slaves and Relationships with Masters (6:1-2)
  II. The Dangers of False Teaching (6:3-10)
  III. A Personal Note to Timothy (6:11-16)
  IV. Concluding Comments About the Rich (6:17-21)

Slaves and Relationships With Masters (6:1-2)

The argument is turned toward slaves who are fortunate enough to have Christian masters. A parallel is drawn between the masters as brothers and as believers. However, with the new impetus of fraternity/ brotherhood, some slaves may be inclined to overstep the bounds of decorum and respect and thus disrupt the household of God. Paul asserts that slaves should be much better servants due to the faith shared with their masters. A similar argument is made in Galatians 5:13.

The Dangers of False Teaching (6:3-10)

Instructions to specific segments of the Christian

population have been instructed in appropriate behavior. Now Paul returns to the thought, and occasionally the exact wording, of 1:3-20.

Teach and urge these duties could refer to the preceding instructions to slaves. However, in the RSV the words begin a new paragraph and are taken to refer to the ensuing discussion regarding false teachings that has dominated the entire letter. For the balance of the letter two concerns are the central focus. First, faithful and unfaithful teachers are characterized. Second, an appropriate attitude toward them is described.

According to some scholars, verse 3 implies some sort of systematized collection of Jesus' sayings against which all teachings must be measured. In at least one other letter Paul makes reference to words attributed to Jesus (see 1 Corinthians 7:10). Acts 20:35 refers to words of the Lord Jesus. These words do not occur in any of the extant Gospels. The idea of appropriate attitude toward riches may be based on Jesus' admonition in the Sermon on the Mount in Matthew 6:24, on Mark 10:23, or on Luke 12:16-21.

The result of teaching that differs from sound teaching is quite clear. The false teachers are arrogant, conceited, and prideful (verse 4). This sort of behavior will only have the effect of splintering the congregation. The vehemence of Paul's outrage suggests that he has a specific individual in mind with whom the congregation will be familiar.

Among the unethical behaviors of false teachers is their inclination to use religion as a means of gain. Two interpretations of this are possible. Recall that preachers and evangelists did have to earn a living and did receive payment for their work. In this letter Paul asserts that executives should be appropriately paid. The emphasis here is that the false teachers may have been inclined to think of their fee as a primary motive for their peculiar religious teaching. They may have been little more than charlatans, willing to play on the sincere religious impulses of unsuspecting believers in order to make a vast profit.

The basic necessities of life are very few. God is characterized as providing for the sojourner the basics (verse 8). Timothy may also hear an allusion to the Sermon on the Mount (see Matthew 6:25).

Using the previously mentioned metaphor of shipwreck (1:19), Paul continues a description of ruin brought on by love of gain and wealth (verse 9). Any focus away from the life to which God summons people through Christ and Christ's teaching carries within it latent peril of personal moral and spiritual disaster.

Verse 10 is often misquoted as "money is the root of all evil." The Scripture reads, *The love of money is the root of all evils.*

A Personal Note to Timothy (6:11-16)

Following the stinging indictment of the personal ethics of false teachers, Paul addresses the young preacher. The designation *man of God* is found only here and in 2 Timothy 3:17. In the Old Testament the designation *man of God* is applied to Moses (Psalm 90:1; Deuteronomy 33:1), prophets (1 Samuel 2:27), Elijah (1 Kings 17:18), and Elisha (2 Kings 4:7). Timothy could hardly have missed the apostle's point. His life is to be considerably different from those of the false teachers.

The young preacher is to pursue basic Christian virtues. THe virtues listed include: (1) attitudes toward God (righteousness, godliness, faith); (2) attitudes toward fellow human beings (love, steadfastness, gentleness); (3) strength to withstand trial; and (4) strength to withstand the virulent attacks of the false teachers.

The conflict between false teaching and sound Christian teaching will not be an easy one. Paul uses a metaphor from sports to illustrate. Paul frequently uses illustrations from athletics. (See 2 Timothy 4:7; 1 Corinthians 9:24;

Philippians 2:16). The notion of the good fight may refer specifically to Timothy's struggle with false teachers. It may also refer to the more general conflict that all Christians will encounter between the claims of Christ and the claims of culture.

Two reasons are given as to why Timothy should persevere in the struggle against the false teachers. First, he has been promised and has claimed eternal life. Eternal life is not an after-death promise. Eternal life begins the moment the individual appropriates the claim and the promise. Second, Timothy must remember his public confession of faith, possibly made at his baptism.

The intensely personal charge to Timothy gathers momentum in verse 13. Only God can give life. Through the presence of God Timothy will be sufficient to the demand as Jesus had been sufficient to the demand of the hour. The reality of the Crucifixion is firmly set in the apostolic preaching of the early church (see Acts 3:13; 4:27; 13:28). Timothy's own confession and courage are to parallel the confession and courage of Jesus before Pilate.

Earlier in his ministry Paul had anticipated an imminent return of Christ (see 1 Thessalonians 5:23). Now, however, he refuses to place a date on the return.

Verse 15b is a description of God's sovereignty over all earthly authority, which begins a sort of doxology.

King of kings and Lord of lords is a phrase found in Deuteronomy 10:17. *Lord of lords* also occurs in Psalm 136:3. In the New Testament the designation is used in Revelation 17:14 and 19:6. These powerful affirmations illustrate clearly the authority that only God has, which exceeds that of any mortal authorities of Pilate's sort.

The notion of *unapproachable light* comes from two sources; Exodus 33:17-23, where Moses seeks to see the glory of God but cannot, and Psalm 104:2. In John's Gospel the evangelist says *No one has ever seen God* (John 1:18; see also 1 John 4:12).

The doxology ends with the traditional *Amen*.

Concluding Comments About the Rich (6:17-21)

Verses 17-19 sound almost anti-climatic after the *Amen* of the doxology. Some scholars suggest that since they are abrupt and unrelated to the preceding verses they have been misplaced from following either verse 2 or 10. Perhaps Paul reflected over his own experience in the Ephesian church, recalling the riot caused by threatened craftsmen during his earlier ministry there (Acts 19:25). Or, the mention of *eternal life* may trigger further reflection on the peril of the love of money.

Paul cannot leave the discussion on a negative note. In verses 18-19 he lists the responsibilities of the economically better-off members of the congregation. Consistent with his advice to other segments of the church (recall 2:10), Paul recommends that the wealthy must be prepared to do good works with their resources. This may include a desire to give to charity (see Romans 12:8; Ephesians 4:28; 1 Corinthians 13:3) or to share with others out of the sheer extravagance of God's own love in which the rich themselves share.

Laying up for themselves a good foundation may be based on the words of Jesus in Matthew 6:20. True life will be theirs if only they will enter into eternal life through love and appropriate hope (see also John 17:3).

The letter concludes in verses 20-21 with personal words from the older apostle to the younger preacher. The conclusion begins with a summation of all that has been argued throughout the letter (1:3-11; 4:1-10; 6:3-10). Timothy has been entrusted with the deposit of faith, the apostolic traditions and teaching.

Grace be with you also occurs in other letters (see 2 Timothy 4:22; Titus 3:15). in the Greek language the word *you* is in the plural. In the English language we would translate it *you all*. Thus tacit acknowledgement, if not instruction, is given that the letter will be read to the entire congregation, in all likelihood in the context of public worship. The blessing is for the entire church.

§ § § § § § §

The Message of 1 Timothy 6

What we believe makes a difference not in the sense that we must be able to present a complete systematized theology of God and Christ, but rather because our theological understandings will eventually be acted out in ethics, attitudes, and behaviors. Paul understands the vital relationship between what we think and how we act. The false teachers' character forms the major part of the final chapter. In sharp contrast to the questionable character of false teachers, the Christian individual lives an exemplary life.

What else can we learn from this chapter?

§ Social status notwithstanding, we are capable of high service in God's name.

§ Our Christian faith leads to better work to the glory of God.

§ Conflicts over petty issues give stark evidence of a lack of Christian faith.

§ The simple gifts of life are to be enjoyed by all Christians.

§ Poor moral decisions can lead to shipwrecked lives.

§ In circumstances requiring courage the Christian can rely on the same power that gave Jesus the courage to maintain his faith.

§ God's authority is greater than any authority on earth.

§ Wealth in itself can be used for good and charity.

§ Dependence on wealth alone may result in missing eternal life that only God can give through Christ.

§ The blessing of Scripture is for the entire church.

§ Diligence and discipline are not options; they are requirements for maintenance of a Christian life.

§ § § § § § §

2 Timothy 1

Introduction to This Chapter

Like the first letter to Timothy, the second letter is a personal letter from the older apostle to a younger colleague. The apostle Paul is imprisoned in Rome (1:8, 16; 2:9). Paul can see the end of the journey rapidly approaching (4:6-8). Therefore, he takes a final opportunity to write to the younger minister with instructions and helpful counsel. The tone of the letter is much more personal than the tone of the first letter.

The Ephesian church still wrestles with the problems created by false teachers. Unlike the first letter, the second letter does not spend as much time laying out the various levels of ministry and qualifications of individuals who would execute those responsibilities. Throughout the letter there is a great deal of concern for the highest possible Christian character.

We cannot determine exactly why the first letter to Timothy precedes the second. One clue may be that the first letter is 113 verses longer than the second, which consists of 83 verses. Another clue may be that the second letter contains a farewell scene beginning in 4:6.

Here is an outline of 2 Timothy 1.

I. Greeting (1:1-2)
II. Paul's Reflections (1:3-5)
III. An Appeal (1:6-18)

Greeting (1:1-2)

In 1 Timothy 1:1 Paul characterizes God's authorization as a commissioning by God. In 2 Timothy he uses the words *by the will of God*. Modern readers may wonder why Paul begins each letter with an affirmation of his authority. Two possibilities emerge. First, Paul may want to establish at the outset the fact that his authority is not merely an authority of permission by a local church. His authority comes primarily from God. Secondly, he may be anticipating a wider reading of personal correspondence. His authority is much more than that granted to him by a trusting colleague.

In 1 Timothy *promise* means the promise of eternal life. Thus in the phrase *according to the promise* Paul alludes not only to his authority but also to the purpose of his apostleship. Titus 1:2 contains a similar promise.

In verse 2 Paul identifies Timothy as a *beloved child*. Similar naming occurs in 1 Corinthians 4:17, *I sent to you Timothy, my beloved and faithful child in the Lord*. In Philippians Paul claims that he has no one like Timothy (Philippians 2:20-22). The implication, therefore, may be that not only does Paul love Timothy as a son, but there is no one else on whom Paul can rely with equal trust. Paul may be speaking over Timothy's shoulder to the listening congregation.

Grace, mercy, and peace recall 1 Timothy 1:2.

Paul's Reflections (1:3-5)

Using a formula common in ancient letters, Paul gives thanks for the individual to whom the letter is addressed. Similar thanksgivings occur in other letters (Romans 1:8-12; 1 and 2 Corinthians; Philippians; and 1 Thessalonians 1:2-3; 3:9). Galatians does not contain such a reflection, probably because the occasion of that writing was hardly a high moment of reverie for a congregation and did not afford the apostle hope and confidence.

When facing the council Paul makes a claim of *clear*

conscience that is similar to that of verse 3 (see Acts 22:30).

The personal expressions of desire to see others (verse 4) occur also in other letters (see 1 Thessalonians 3:6). In Romans 1:11 Paul wishes to visit with the Roman church in order to *impart to you some spiritual gift to strengthen you.* In comparison to these statements, the longing here appears even more personal, in part because Paul includes allusion to the tearful departure at Miletus (Acts 20:37).

Three times in the letter Paul expresses his desire that Timothy come to visit him (see 4:9, 21). The reminder of tears evokes strong desire to be filled with joy. Similar coincidences of joy and tears occur in other letters as well. In 2 Corinthians Paul declares, *I rejoice, not because you were grieved, but because you were grieved into repenting* (2 Corinthians 7:9). In Philippians Paul courageously confesses, *Even if I am to be poured as a libation upon the sacrificial offering of your faith, I am glad and rejoice with you all* (Philippians 2:17). Both our tears and our laughter express soul-felt emotions, and are intimately related.

In verse 5, Paul's rejoicing is triggered by either a memory or an actual piece of news regarding Timothy's faith. Perhaps he has recently received news, *because we have heard of your faith in Christ Jesus and of the love which you have for all the saints* (Colossians 1:4). In either event, the source of rejoicing is Timothy's *sincere faith.* Some commentators question Paul's use of *faith* in this context. In at least one other instance Paul does question the sincerity of faith in another (see 1 Thessalonians 3:5). The implication in verse 5 is that Timothy's faith is one that he has expressed publicly and one that is largely internalized as well, since he has learned it from both his grandmother and his mother.

Lois and Eunice were the first Christians in Timothy's family (Acts 16:1). Paul has already reflected on his own Jewish tradition with thanksgiving. Here he celebrates the tradition that has informed Timothy's own faith.

An Appeal (1:6-18)

Verses 6-8 serve as a transition linking the trajectory of Timothy's faith with the current demand for courage and strength.

In verse 6 the image of smoldering embers serves as an appropriate metaphor. Timothy must stir up into white-hot heat his internalized faith.

The word for *gift* is *charisma*, a special gift or power given by God. Here the gift is closely linked with Timothy's ordination, that is, the laying on of hands (recall 1 Timothy 4:14). This may be a reference to Paul's initial choice of Timothy as a minister (Acts 16:3). Moreover, the letter's public reading would remind any and all ordained individuals of the special gift that had been bestowed upon them at their own ordinations. Thus the letter serves the larger purpose of stirring all ministers' gifts.

The gifts of God (verse 7) are not merely human attributes inherent within the best and brightest. These endowments, including power, love, and self-control, are gifts from God and are directly related to the specific demand of the current circumstance.

Power here means the power of the gospel itself, a moral power sufficient for any and all circumstances. *I am not ashamed of the Gospel: it is the power of God for salvation* (Romans 1:16). Paul refers to his own anxiety when he first ministered in Corinth (1 Corinthians 2:4). In other correspondence to the Corinthians Paul declares his intention to demonstrate the difference between mere human power and God's power (see 1 Corinthians 4:19-20).

First John 4:18 points to a *love* that has great power. *There is no fear in love, but perfect love casts out fear.*

Self-discipline (here only in the New Testament) is the capacity to keep one's head when all around want to go to extremes. In short, a Christian minister must be able to keep control of his or her temper.

Note Paul's gracious inclusion of himself as one of the persons receiving God's gifts. Even if he is reprimanding the younger minister for his having allowed the gift to grow cold, Paul takes the sharp edge off his criticism.

Evidently Paul himself at one point considered the possibility of being ashamed of the gospel. *I am not ashamed of the gospel* (Romans 1:16). In verse 8, however, instead of concealing his own potential embarrassment behind the cloak of condescension or arrogance, he has learned compassion for others who at some point may share his own momentary hesitation or anxiety.

Timothy is already up against strong resistance. Now he has to give witness to the gospel of a crucified Messiah, *a stumbling block to Jews and a folly to Gentiles* (1 Corinthians 1:23). Worse yet, his mentor and higher authority, Paul, is himself a prisoner, chained as a common criminal. Timothy is not the first to experience real stress due to Paul's imprisonment. *For this reason I, Paul, a prisoner for Christ Jesus on behalf of you Gentiles* (Ephesians 3:1). In Philippians Paul apologizes for what must have troubled or embarrassed fellow Christians. *I want you to know, brethren, that what has happened to me has really served to advance the gospel* (Philippians 1:12). In his letter to Philemon, Paul begins by calling himself *a prisoner for Christ Jesus.* But Paul illustrates his remarkable faith by reframing his imprisonment from something of which to be ashamed into something that draws even more attention to the power of God and the gospel. Incredibly, Paul invites the reluctant minister to join with him in the sufferings for the gospel.

Is Paul suggesting that only when one is willing to endure the sufferings can one truly know the immensity of God's power?

Quickly following a remarkable invitation, the letter continues (verses 9-10) with what may be short citations of familiar liturgical material. Perhaps Paul has anticipated the younger minister's questions and hesitation. In rapid succession the peculiar powers that are available only to Christians are enumerated.

The term *savior* is used to describe God five times in the Pastoral Epistles (1 Timothy 1:1; 2:3; 4:10; Titus 2:10; 3:4). The term is used four times to describe Christ (here and in Titus 1:4; 2:13; 3:6).

God calls through no human virtue but rather only by God's own initiative. *To the church of God . . . to those sanctified in Christ Jesus, called to be saints* (1 Corinthians 1:2), or again, *called to be saints* (Romans 1:7). And the call is to be a holy people, *for God has not called us for uncleanness, but in holiness* (1 Thessalonians 4:7).

The call of God marks an initial stage in the process of salvation, *and those whom he predestined he also called; and those whom he called he also justified; and those whom he justified he also glorified* (Romans 8:30).

God calls for God's own purposes. Paul makes a similar declaration to the Christians in Rome (Romans 8:28).

God's purpose was not discovered by humankind. Instead, God's purpose has existed even before Creation itself in the imagination and intention of God for the entire creation. Ephesians 1:4 holds to a pre-existent Christ in whom grace is embodied. However, God's grace will not be discernible until it is revealed through and in the midst of real history with a human face on it.

The human face of God is our Savior Christ Jesus. Interestingly, Jesus never used the term *Savior* for himself.

Paul continues by describing the saving work of Jesus. Consistent with other declarations, Paul affirms first that Jesus has *abolished death* (see 1 Corinthians 15:26, 55). Jesus accomplished this work through the teaching of eternal life and also by the overwhelming truth of the Resurrection, *for thou wilt not abandon my soul to Hades, nor let thy Holy One see corruption* (Acts 2:27). The letter to the Hebrews captures the dramatic importance of this truth as well (see Hebrews 2:14-15). In no small way should we overlook the prominent placement of this work in Paul's list. Timothy has been summoned to face the possibility of death courageously.

Second, Paul affirms that Jesus has *brought life and immortality to light.* In the Greek language immortality means incorruptibility that only God can bestow: *To those who by patience in well-doing seek for glory and honor and immortality, he will give eternal life* (Romans 2:7). Without an actual historical event we would never have known of God's action. Recall that at least a part of the false teachings with which Timothy must wrestle is an emphasis on myths. Part of the genius of both the Old and New Testaments is that history is treated with great respect, as it is the arena in which God's work is carried out.

At the mention of the gospel, Paul exults in a series of personal reflections regarding the importance of the gospel in his own life. Indeed, he had been appointed a *preacher, apostle,* and *teacher* (see 1 Corinthians 12:28). This is not an attempt to further establish Paul's authority in the life of the young preacher or the church. Rather, the sense is one of firm conviction that along with the appointment to these high authorities there is a high responsibility: Paul must *suffer* (verse 12).

However, Paul refuses to languish in his suffering. For him, suffering is part and parcel of the gospel itself. In this manner the younger preacher is shown a dual task of the preacher. First is the well-known and readily accepted model as proclaimer and teacher. The second is more subtle, yet threatening: The preacher must in one sense be a model of suffering for the entire church. How can the old apostle bear up under duress? From his own experience, he has been able to entrust to God all that is important to him, including his teaching (see 1 Corinthians 3:12-15), his preaching, and his converts (see Acts 20:32). Paul has learned through personal experience that God is trustworthy with all of life. Moreover, as Paul himself has guarded the apostolic tradition and teaching, so God will continue to watch over the entrustment (the deposit of faith).

The meaning is deliberately ambiguous. The church has been entrusted with the deposit of the tradition, the deposit of faith. By the same token the church has entrusted itself (individually and collectively) to God. In both interpretations faithfulness and trustworthiness characterize the relationship and responsibility. The significance of this statement cannot be lost on the younger minister, Timothy.

In verse 13 Paul returns to the theme of verse 8, that is, sound teaching (recall 1 Timothy 1:10). Timothy's ministry is not merely one of words and proclamation. His ministry is to be one of personal model (recall 1 Timothy 1:16) and example, even in the midst of extremely threatening circumstances.

Where will this Christian preacher under fire find sufficient strength for this sort of courageous life? No preacher will have the resources solely from sheer moral grit (see Romans 8:9, 11). Paul affirms in verse 14 that the indwelling presence of the Holy Spirit will be sufficient. No doubt the message is also intended for the entire church's hearing. The same power is present with *all* Christians.

In verses 15-18 Paul illustrates his point with negative examples. He lists individuals who have failed in keeping the faith.

Asia means the Roman province consisting of Mysia, Lydia, Caria, large portions of Phrygia, and the offshore islands. The capital of the region is Ephesus.

Evidently Timothy is familiar with the circumstances and individuals of whom Paul speaks. Presumably the other Christians overhearing this letter are aware of these facts as well. At least one scholar contends that Paul's exaggeration of *all Asia* (after all, he mentions only a handful of individuals and hardly an entire region) illustrates typical symptoms of depression. More to the point, Paul uses exaggeration in order to prove that no one will be sufficient on his or her own and not all will be able to pass the trial by fire.

We cannot determine the exact nature of the turning away. The men could have abandoned correct doctrine as implied by the preceding two verses. The same verb is used that describes doctrinal error (Titus 1:14). However, since this statement is couched in laudatory terms for Onesiphorus, it is equally possible that the men refused to stand with Paul during his trial.

We know nothing about Phygelos and Hermogenes. Onesiphorus is mentioned later in 4:19 as one whose family lives in Ephesus. According to one legend he was a citizen of Iconium and had been converted to Christianity by Paul during a missionary journey.

The phrase *May the Lord grant . . . mercy* is used only here in the New Testament.

Paul's argument can hardly be lost on Timothy or the congregation. Onesiphorus was in no sense ashamed of Paul's imprisonment. Indeed, he sought out the apostle in Rome. This may sound very peculiar to us. But in Acts the narrative states clearly that Paul had relative freedom during his imprisonment (Acts 28:30-31). If Onesiphorus is unashamed of the chains, then Timothy (and others) should not be ashamed of them.

The chapter concludes in verse 18 with a short prayer on behalf of Onesiphorus. The prayer is intercessory, not daring to lay claim on the graces of God, but sincerely requesting God's gracious actions toward this helping man. Since the term *on that Day* suggests judgment, often associated with the final judgment, scholars conclude that this may be an early Christian appropriation of the Jewish tradition of prayers for the dead.

By implication the chapter's final scene is the Christian preacher and church reflecting on the life of a man and circumstances that they knew well.

§ § § § § § §

The Message of 2 Timothy 1

The Christian gospel that both the old apostle and the younger preacher are called to preach is sometimes a scorned and attacked gospel. In this chapter Timothy is summoned to a courageous witness that gives actual life to an ideal. However, the chapter is not mere exhortation to moral effort. Once again, God is characterized as life-giver and sustainer. The model life is possible only because God remains present with the person through the power of the Holy Spirit.

What else can we learn from this chapter?

§ All Christians are indebted to others for their faith; we learn from our families; we inherit the tradition.

§ Christians need to stir their gifts, lest they become cold and unused.

§ The gospel may be potentially embarrassing; however, the gospel is one of power and therefore we should not be ashamed of it.

§ God's intention for the creation has been in God's imagination from before time itself.

§ Christ has defeated death and the fear of death.

§ Trust and responsibility are both God's and ours.

§ In times of crisis many may fail; few will sustain courageous moral life.

§ We should never overlook the power of one life and the difference that one life can make.

§ § § § § § §

2 Timothy 2

Introduction to This Chapter

Chapter 2 consists of two sets of instructions. The first is a series of instructions regarding Timothy's own disciplines. The second set has to do with Timothy's responsibilities to teachers.

Here is an outline of this chapter.

I. Instructions to Timothy (2:1-13)
   A. Hand on teaching to others (2:1-2)
   B. Be ready for suffering, endure (2:3-7)
   C. Theological undergirding (2:8-10)
   D. A citation from a hymn (2:11-13)
II. Instructions Regarding the Teachers (2:14-26)
   A. Beware of empty arguments (2:14)
   B. Set a personal example (2:15-19)
   C. Aim at central virtues (2:20-23)
   D. Characteristics of the Lord's servant (2:24-26)

Instructions to Timothy (2:1-13)

Chapter 2 continues an exhortation to courage that began in 1:8. *Do not be ashamed then of testifying to our Lord . . . but share in suffering for the gospel in the power of God.* The exhortation continues through this chapter to its conclusion in 4:8.

Hand On Teaching to Others (2:1-2)

Paul had identified two dismal failures and lifted one individual up for prayer at the conclusion of the previous chapter. The present chapter begins by placing Timothy into sharp contrast with the previously mentioned failures: *You then.*

Timothy is encouraged to *be strong.* The Greek word can also be translated *be empowered,* a favorite word of Paul's that is used six times in other writings. Paul refers to Abraham's courage. *No distrust made him waver concerning the promise of God, but he grew strong in his faith* (Romans 4:20). To the Philippians Paul declares, *I can do all things in him who strengthens me* (Philippians 4:13). The Ephesians are exhorted to *be strong in the Lord and in the strength of his might* (Ephesians 6:10). But the strength is not a matter of sheer grit on Timothy's part. Instead, the strength to which Paul refers is the strength that comes through the grace and power of Christ Jesus.

Verse 2 states that from Timothy's own experience, both in learning from Paul and personal experience of trial-tested confirmation, he is to *teach others.*

Many witnesses may be an allusion to Timothy's ordination. These others could also be presbyters (recall 1 Timothy 4:14) or others who heard Paul preach. In 1 Corinthians 15:3-11 Paul refers to his own faithfulness to the apostolic gospel as he received it from many others. *For I delivered to you as of first importance what I also received* (verse 3). Then he lists individuals and groups of people who can give witness to the truth of the gospel. Furthermore, Timothy must be extremely careful in selecting the best people to carry the responsibility of passing on the faith to others.

Be Ready for Suffering, Endure (2:3-7)

In verses 3-7 three metaphors follow in rapid succession. Each of the images suggests the intensity and discipline that Christian leaders will have to maintain. In this context Paul applies them especially to Christian ministers, as he does in 1 Corinthians 9:7, 24-27.

The images suggest two major concerns: (a)

wholehearted devotion to the purposes of the minister and (b) the hope of a reward. The soldier must be of a single purpose and detached from other concerns. His predominant motive is to please his superior officers. The implication for the Christian minister is clear. The minister needs to consider his work with the same singular purpose and with only the thought of pleasing God (see 1 Corinthians 7:32). The same imperative is affirmed in 1 John 3:22.

The athlete competes according to established rules of the competition. No competitor can expect to do well without training and self-discipline. Here the older apostle subtly points toward the personal preparation of the minister. In the critical moments of stress and threat, the minister can only draw on what has been internalized through the disciplines of study and prayer.

In the agricultural image, Paul makes the transition from the arduous disciplines to the rewards that the worker may anticipate.

The RSV translation of verse 7, *Think over what I say*, may also be more forcefully translated, *Think out my meaning*, which carries with it a much stronger connotation. To the Corinthians Paul had made a similar charge, *I speak as to sensible men; judge for yourselves what I say* (1 Corinthians 10:15). Timothy and others like him will have to determine for themselves the truth of what Paul has already discovered in his own life. Ultimately Timothy will have to live on the basis of what he himself knows to be true. Paul has subtly assigned the responsibility for learning to Timothy.

However, Timothy will not have to work on his own. Paul knows that the Lord Jesus will give Timothy insight and wisdom (see 1 Corinthians 3:10, 13, 15).

Theological Undergirding (2:8-10)

The affirmations about Jesus Christ in verse 8 sound like creedal statements and may indeed be excerpts from early Christian formulations, especially the affirmation of Jesus' genealogy.

Only here in the Pastoral Epistles does Paul refer to *Jesus Christ*. The usual order is *Christ Jesus*. The reversal is not accidental. By mentioning Jesus first, Paul draws immediate attention to the historic life of the human Jesus who lived as we live, and who died on the cross. Paul could thus be lifting up before Timothy the necessity and inevitability of the way of the cross. The cross of Christ has cast its shadow across Timothy's path.

The Resurrection means much more than the fact that on the first day of the week the tomb was empty. The towering fact is that the risen Lord will be with Timothy as life-giving power.

Preached in my gospel opens up three alternative interpretations. To begin with, Paul asserts that the gospel is not of his own design or invention. Indeed, a gospel with the cross of suffering at its center can hardly be merely a human invention. Furthermore, this statement implies the existence of an established or orthodox definition of what the Christian faith is, that is, the apostolic faith with which Paul has been entrusted (recall 1 Timothy 1:11). The statement also makes the assertion that the gospel is no gospel until it is personally appropriated by the individual. Paul makes the same assertion to the Roman church (in Romans 2:16 and again in Romans 16:25). Modern readers may be offended by what appears to be an audacious claim by the apostle. However, Paul knows by hard-wrought personal experience that the only gospel is one that has been proven adequate through the very real stresses of authentic ministry in unfamiliar and hostile surroundings.

In verse 9, the gospel is the reason that Paul goes through the humiliation of public censure and imprisonment as a common criminal. Scholars have found that this usage reflects a time of official state persecution.

Even in the most hostile surroundings the word of God is not chained. While Paul has been imprisoned, others have continued preaching and teaching the gospel. While imprisoned, Paul wrote to the Philippians daring to claim that what had happened was really for the purpose of advancing the gospel (see Philippians 1:12-14). The Old Testament prophet Isaiah first made such a claim (see (Isaiah 55:11).

The authentic gospel of Christ as preached by the apostle Paul has a cross and sufferings as well as the glory of an eternal inheritance at its center. Paul weaves his own sufferings into the tapestry of the gospel, thus making sense out of his and potentially others' sufferings. Sufferings in this sense are not mere accidents of history or the result of evil design by government.

Explaining further in verse 10, Paul states that his sufferings are a part of his evangelism. Sufferings serve in the work of spearheading the gospel. He suffers so that all may receive the news of salvation which is only in Christ Jesus. The primitive Christian church believed that suffering would have to precede the ultimate victory of God's intention. *When you hear of wars and rumors of wars, do not be alarmed; this must take place, but the end is not yet* (Mark 13:7). In Luke 21 Jesus responds to the urgent questioning of the disciples regarding the end time. Included in Jesus' description is the cold truth, *they will lay their hands on you and persecute you, delivering you up to the synagogues and prisons, and you will be brought before kings and governors for my name's sake. By your endurance you will gain your lives* (verses 12, 19).

A Citation From a Hymn (2:11-13)

This section concludes with a trustworthy saying (recall 1 Timothy 1:15; 3:1; 4:9. A similar usage occurs in Titus 3:8). The saying refers to verses 11-13 that follow, excerpts from a Christian hymn.

The hymn consists of four strophes, the first three of

which contain parallel affirmations. *If we have died . . . we shall live; if we endure . . . we shall reign; if we deny . . . he will deny.* The fourth strophe contains a remarkable affirmation of God's faithfulness, *if we are faithless . . . he remains faithful.*

The first strophe may stem from Paul's earlier affirmation regarding the Christian's baptismal confession, *if we have died with Christ, we believe that we shall also live with him* (Romans 6:8). In Colossians 3:3 Paul makes a similar claim, again referring to the sacrament of baptism.

If we deny him picks up on the theme of Matthew 10:32-33 (see also Mark 8:38; Luke 12:9).

Quickly the hymn moves from the past (death) to (the future) victorious eternal life. Endurance is necessary for those who will reign with Christ.

In what may be a surprising statement, the hymn concludes with the ringing affirmation that even if Christians cannot endure, still God remains faithful, for it is the very character of God to remain faithful to God's promises. Romans 3:3-4 contains a similar affirmation. The final affirmation is not to be misconstrued as permission for laxity. God is good to the promise both of blessing and curse, reward and punishment. (See also Exodus 34:6-7.) The Christian must maintain the delicate balance between accepting forgiveness and arrogantly flaunting iniquity.

Every individual has known at least one moment when he or she wanted to say, "That wasn't me." We act out of character due either to stress, weariness, or simply a lack of diligence in an unguarded moment. Surely Timothy or others listening could recall all too vividly an unguarded moment when courageous and exemplary witness was disregarded. What then? Will God seize the moment to curse and condemn? The biblical insight is that God is incapable of acting out of character. To underscore this point, the earliest Christian hymns celebrated the utter consistency of God.

Instructions Regarding the Teachers (2:14-26)

Beginning with verse 14, the chapter shifts the focus from Timothy to the teachers with whom the faith will be entrusted, from the character of what will be taught to the character of the teachers themselves. Paul further emphasizes the need for sound teaching (recall his emphasis in 1:12-14; 2:1-3) through a reminder to preach the gospel (summarized in verses 11-13) as received and learned through the apostle (2:2).

While this section is very much like 1 Timothy 4:6-16, significant differences should be noted. A strong contrast is drawn between work and words, between true speech and false speech.

Beware of Empty Arguments (2:14)

The teachers must be reminded to keep their hearers' best interest in mind. Therefore, teachers should be advised most solemnly not to fritter away valuable time in disputes that can never be resolved. The point is not to avoid debate altogether. Instead the point is that teachers should not waste time with debates not intrinsically related to the life-giving truths of the Christian gospel.

Set a Personal Example (2:15-19)

The means by which the preacher will affect the desired result in the teachers is by his own personal model, that is, by example. The way to good preaching and teaching requires three steps: First is hard work, the second is more hard work, and the third is still more hard work. If nothing else, then, Timothy can see to it that he is at least a sound workman with *no need to be ashamed*. To the Roman congregation Paul had made similar charges (see Romans 6:13). One of the tenets of biblical faith is submission of oneself to God for judgment (1 Corinthians 3:12-13). Continuing with what may be another illustration from stonemasonry, Paul indicates that the preacher should, like the stonecutter, cut straight, that is, handle properly, the awesome task of interpreting the word.

At the center of the preacher's work is the *word of truth* that can be interpreted either of two ways. The first is the word as the gospel itself (Colossians 1:5) and *the word of truth, the gospel of your salvation* (Ephesians 1:13). The second, equally valid, translation is Scripture as the written word of the gospel. One commentator contends that to make any attempt to further define what Paul instructed is to play into the same hand that Paul counsels Timothy to avoid, namely, to enter into endless and unresolvable debate.

False teachers lead themselves and their followers away from rather than toward the center of godliness (recall 1 Timothy 4:15). Worse yet, their talk is like *gangrene* spreading further into the body of the church.

In verse 17, two of the false teachers are mentioned by name. Philetus appears only here in the entire New Testament. Hymenaeus was mentioned earlier (1 Timothy 1:20). Why is this man mentioned a second time? Some scholars contend that this letter should actually be the first letter sent. But we cannot prove this beyond conjecture. What can be ascertained by implication is that the circumstances in the Ephesian church reached such a state that even the authority of the Apostle Paul took quite some time to have an effect.

These two false teachers have *swerved from the truth* (verse 18). Only here does Paul give specific insight into the teaching of the false teachers. Their error has to do with the Resurrection. Contrary to Christian doctrine, which holds to a bodily resurrection (Romans 6:5), they have taught that the resurrection is only a spiritual resurrection for the Christian that takes place at the time of baptism. Thus the Christian faith is made into something akin to a development from one moral level to another, higher, moral level. This teaching shows Gnostic influence that held to a notion of a higher knowledge.

In other correspondence, Paul recognizes the essential significance of the resurrection (see, for example, 1 Corinthians 15:12-14). Paul knows from his own bitter experience the sort of havoc that has been inflicted on people's faith by false teachers.

However, in verse 19, against the apparent authority of the false teachers, God's authority will prevail. We see the image of a firm foundation of apostles and prophets with Jesus Christ himself as the cornerstone.

On the cornerstone a seal or an inscription of some kind would have been inscribed, indicating its ownership, its purpose, or the stonemason's identity. Paul quotes two sayings with which Timothy is no doubt familiar. The first may be taken from Numbers 16:5, making the point that in the final analysis God will be able to determine who has been loyal and who has been disloyal or false to the faith. *The Lord knows* may also be a statement that God has thorough insight into the inner person and knows each individual better than the individual himself or herself does.

The second saying has its roots in the Old Testament as well (see Leviticus 24:16 and Isaiah 26:13).

In the Old Testament one narrative stands out as the illustration of apostasy. Numbers 16 contains the story of the rebellion of Korah against Moses. Also, Jude 11 alludes to the incident.

Aim at Central Virtues (2:20-23)

The predominant metaphor of the family or household returns in verse 20 (recall 1 Timothy 3:5, 15). Timothy is counseled to be tolerant of different sorts of individuals in the church. Paul had to wrestle with the same stresses in the Corinthian church (see 1 Corinthians 12:20-27). To the Romans Paul posed the question, *Has the potter no right over the clay, to make out of the same lump one vessel for beauty and another for menial use?* (Romans 9:21).

Tolerance of something is one thing; association and

identification with it are yet another. In verse 21, Timothy is told to keep his distance from any false teachers, for they can still exert baser moral influence on him.

The discussion regarding the preacher's exemplary discipline, that had been interrupted after verse 16, is resumed in verse 22. Paul combines the thoughts of 1 Timothy 4:12 and 1 Timothy 6:11.

Timothy must come to terms with the impulses that haunt the younger minister, and foster the opposite impulses of *righteousness, patience, faith, love,* and *peace.* The younger man may have exhibited impulses of confrontation to the point of self-assertion, perhaps with a measure of self-indulgence as well. All of these characteristics affect relationships with others.

Timothy is reminded that the church fellowship is the best environment in which to aim at and foster the high virtues of the Christian faith.

Those who call on the Lord may also be an allusion to the worship life of the congregation. Thus, Timothy is reminded of the teaching ministry of worship itself.

Unstructured questioning, translated in the RSV as *stupid, senseless controversies,* occurs only here in the New Testament.

Characteristics of the Lord's Servant (2:24-26)

The Lord's servant in verse 24 implies especially the minister, *a servant of Jesus Christ* (Romans 1:1); *Paul and Timothy, servants of Christ Jesus* (Philippians 1:1). The image is drawn from the servant images in the prophet Isaiah (42:1-4 and 52:13–53:12).

The characteristics of the servant of the Lord are listed. In short, the minister is to be like Christ in winning people to the gospel.

What are Christlike characteristics? A servant is *kindly to everyone* (recall Paul's own attitude toward the Thessalonians, expressed in 1 Thessalonians 2:7)—*an apt teacher,* both patient and understanding.

In verse 25, nothing is to be gained when the teacher becomes impatient and abusive toward the students/learners. In teaching, the teacher's method is as important as the content. The Christian teacher not only teaches grace, but also lives graciously. The moral example of the teacher may itself be a tool of evangelism.

The Greek word for *repent* is *metanoia*, meaning a turning around or an about face. Acknowledgement of the truth means conversion to the Christian faith.

Conversion to the truth is but half the victory. The other half is avoidance of the snare set by the evil one (recall 1 Timothy 3:7). Verse 26 poses difficulties in interpretation due to the awkward pronouns. Has the individual been ensnared by the devil to do his will? or to the Lord and the Lord's will? The best understanding is to see the individual ensnared by the devil but captured by God, through conversion, to do God's will. This reading concludes the chapter on a note of hope and great encouragement for Timothy and his congregation.

§ § § § § § § §

The Message of 2 Timothy 2

Little did Timothy realize at his ordination that he would someday be appointed to such a difficult church. Threatened by false teachers, he must contend with the apparent authority these false teachers have garnered for themselves. But in the conflict he must keep in mind that his style has as much influence as, if not more than, his doctrinal correctness.

What else can we learn from this chapter?

§ The Christian life is a life of disciplines and exclusive concentration.

§ Embedded in the Christian gospel is suffering for the gospel.

§ The gospel must be accepted if it is to be a living gospel.

§ No matter what the circumstances, God's word cannot be chained or contained.

§ God's nature is to remain faithful to God's promises, even through the failure of God's people.

§ Good preaching and teaching are not accidental; they require diligent effort.

§ Against apparent authority of challenges, God's authority through Christ will prevail.

§ In the church we can expect all sorts of people—brighter lights, lesser lights, persons of noble calling, and others of humble gifts.

§ The church is the best environment in which to learn and foster the highest ideals and moral/spiritual values.

§ Teachers must have an essential integrity in both method and content.

§ People may be drawn to the gospel through our actions rather than our words.

§ § § § § § § §

PART NINE

2 Timothy 3

Introduction to This Chapter

Chapter 3 continues the call to courageous living in a time when heretics will have increasing appeal. This section is closely related in thought to 1 Timothy 4:1-5. All of Chapter 3 is placed in the context of the last days. The reflections in this chapter are an analysis of the stress that Paul actually sees in the Ephesian church. The current stresses with which Timothy must contend, then, are actual occurrences of what had been predicted in earlier Christian writings.

Here is an outline of this chapter.

I. Toward an Uncertain Future (3:1-9)
   A. Times will get more difficult (3:1)
   B. Even Christians will waver (3:2-5)
   C. False teachers will have their day (3:6-9)
II. Remain Loyal to the Faith (3:10-17)
   A. Timothy has a guide (3:10-14)
   B. Timothy has Scripture (3:15-17)

Toward an Uncertain Future (3:1-9)

All three synoptic Gospels contain Jesus' own prediction that there will be a time of incredible stress for the Christian. Matthew 24:4-44 and Luke 21:5-37 parallel Mark 13:3-37. In all three Jesus answers the disciples' question regarding the end time, *Tell us, when will this be, and what will be the sign when these things are all to be accomplished?* Predictions of false teachers leading people astray, wars and rumors of wars, persecutions, and families rent asunder paint a dismal and desperate picture of general religious upheaval and apostasy characterized by the emergence of false leaders.

Times Will Get More Difficult (3:1)

Paul instructs Timothy to recognize what is happening as fulfillment of what has been predicted. The days before the Parousia are here. These days will be difficult, and teachers and preachers will have a hard time living by the high principles listed in 2:24-26. To the Ephesian church in another letter, Paul advised Christians to make the most of their time, even though the *days are evil* (Ephesians 5:16). Outward circumstances cannot prevent the Christian from using time wisely.

Even Christians Will Waver (3:2-5)

The circumstances in Ephesus show that times of stress have already begun. A similar list appears in Romans 1:29-31. Presumably Paul means all people, not only men, will fall prey to the spirit of the time.

Self-loving means that people have replaced self for God. They have lost the true center of life and replaced it with ego. The results are quite predictable: Any larger sense of duty or responsibility to God and others is lost.

Lovers of money recalls a similar observation in 1 Timothy 6:10 where the love of money is considered the source of all evil. Here the love of money is not so much the source of evil as the symptom of a displaced God. James addresses the same issue (see James 5:3).

Pride and arrogance are two more evidences of a displaced God. Men and women are inclined to boast about their own gifts, especially to those who are apparently less gifted. Jesus criticized this attitude when he observed an arrogant Pharisee at prayer (Luke 18:9-14), *God, I thank thee that I am not like other men* (verse 11). Equally as dangerous is the disciples' inclination to feel a certain pride in the fact that they are not like the criticized Pharisee. The latent peril of pride is not a Pharisee problem or false teacher problem. The peril of pride is thoroughly and universally human. By implication, the boasters are also arrogant toward God.

Deeply rooted in the Old Testament (see the fifth commandment in the Ten Commandments), and continuing into the Christian church is respect for parents. To the Ephesians Paul writes, *Children, obey your parents in the Lord, for this is right. "Honor your father and your mother" (this is the first commandment with a promise)* (Ephesians 6:1-2). Maintaining the integrity of the family/household is central in Timothy's work. Recall that the theme of the family/household is a recurrent image in the Pastoral Epistles (1 Timothy 5:4; Titus 1:6). The Greek term that the RSV translates *disobedient* can also be translated *abusive*, which carries a much stronger connotation.

The word *implacable* may be enlarged to include an inability to keep one's word. The impression is of an individual who simply cannot get along with or come to terms with anyone else.

Slanderers may include individuals who purposely set one person against another in order to gain, even if only through the discord and disruption.

Reckless means hasty or without regard for consequences of speech or action. Perhaps Paul has in mind the speech during the near-riot he witnessed in Ephesus in which wise counsel carried the hour (see Acts 19:36).

Conceit among false teachers is frequently mentioned (recall 1 Timothy 3:6; 6:4).

The scathing list concludes with a summary in parallel with verse 2 that false teachers love pleasure rather than God. This summary serves as a closing bracket to the list. Given this formidable list of indictments, why would any Christian minister have to be concerned about losing people to the authority of false teachers? Surely such behavior and attitudes are obvious.

The chapter continues with what may be an anticipation of just such a protest. The false teachers are not altogether evil on first sight. Indeed, they seem to have all the outward appearances of religion. They can recite the orthodox creeds (see Romans 2:20), as well as provide a worship service that corresponds to the Christian worship service. The real failure of the false teachers is not their lack of religion. Their failure is that their religion is all form and no life-giving substance. Paul confesses to the Corinthian congregation that he does not want their faith to rest on anything as insubstantial as an apparent wisdom of his own (see 1 Corinthians 2:5).

False Teachers Will Have Their Day (3:6-9)

Modern readers may be quick to read the following counsel to mean that they should avoid this sort of person altogether. However, recall that in earlier counsel Paul had told the younger minister to maintain a basic pastoral concern and relationship with all individuals, including the offending individuals, with the hope that they may repent and come to the faith.

The real challenge will be retaining an attitude that is not affected by the false teachers, while at the same time maintaining some sort of valid relationship in which moral persuasion by the Christian may have an effect.

Recall that Paul himself had first met women in several of his journeys. Having made the initial contact with women, he frequently found himself invited into the home. Unfortunately for the young minister Timothy, the tactics of false teachers are precisely those of a healthy Christian evangelism. The false teachers make their way into homes where the women are particularly open to the new religious offering.

When people feel that they are trapped in their lives, they will reach to religion, even false religion, with the desperation of a drowning person reaching for a branch.

The false teachers are also difficult to identify immediately, since they give the impression of desiring to learn. However, they can be easily identified later, since they (1) do not want to learn seriously; they are only attracted to novelty, and (2) exhibit no real capacity to be changed by their learning. They cannot reach the *knowledge of the truth*, meaning Christian conversion and faith (recall 2:25 and 1 Timothy 2:4).

Jannes and Jambres in verse 8 are figures associated with Moses. Jewish tradition holds that they were the magicians who confronted Moses (Exodus 7:11; 9:11). Their names do not appear in the Old Testament narrative. We should not be surprised that a very specific reference is made to the Mosaic tradition. The earliest Christians were after all, trained in their earlier lives as good, religious Jews. The New Testament assumes a literacy among Christians. In Stephen's speech Moses is mentioned (Acts 7:22). Paul alludes to Moses in 1 Corinthians 10:1-2.

Paul may be arguing against the practice of magic. But the flow of the argument has more to do with the manner in which the false teachers have perverted the teachings of the faith and the susceptible minds of vulnerable people.

According to verse 9 the false teachers will have their hour. They will make some inroads and achieve apparent victory. However, over the long haul they will be discovered for what they are. Rather than remaining figures of victory, they will become little more than a laughingstock for all who see their folly. Paul's counsel is that evil has within it the seeds of its own destruction. With regard to evangelistic efforts of false teachers, the greatest authority is not a countering combat by the Christian preacher. The greatest authority for the Christian faith is moral example (the power of religion) and the lack of real power among false teachers.

Timothy Has a Guide (3:10-14)

The thought of false teachers' apparent authority triggers a personal reflection in verse 10. Paul alludes to the authority of his own experience, perhaps to remind Timothy of what he himself saw as he accompanied Paul during earlier missionary work. Timothy had himself been witness to Paul's teaching (see 1 Corinthians 4:17).

In addition to the mention of *sufferings*, specific cities in which he suffered are listed: Antioch of Pisidia (Acts 13:14-52), Iconium (Acts 14:1-20), and Lystra (Acts 16:1-5).

To the Corinthians Paul illustrates the central significance of sufferings and Paul's response to them (see 2 Corinthians 6:4-5). The same theme occurs in 2 Corinthians 11:24-28.

Paul's own witness is that through it all, God has been sufficient to deliver him from ultimate harm in every circumstance. Is Paul suggesting to a timid Timothy that in whatever circumstance the younger minister finds himself, God will be sufficient for him as well? Furthermore, Timothy cannot expect to do the work of Christian witness without evoking antagonism.

Paul continues in verse 12 almost without taking a breath: *All who desire to live a godly life . . . will be persecuted*! Little doubt can persist—being Christian will carry with it a sentence of some suffering. If anyone should claim the title of Christian, Paul will invoke the authority of his own suffering (see also 2 Corinthians 11:23). To the Thessalonians Paul suggests a reminder, *For when we were with you, we told you beforehand that we were to suffer affliction; just as it has come to pass, and as you know* (1 Thessalonians 3:4). During the return journey through Lystra, Iconium, and Antioch, Paul preached and encouraged all Christians, *exhorting them to continue in the faith, and saying that through many tribulations we must enter the kingdom of God* (Acts 14:22).

To live a *godly life in Christ Jesus* is to incorporate one's ego into Christ (see Romans 6:11).

In this context *evil men* and *deceivers* are deliberately malicious individuals purposely setting out to persecute others. Paul uses their own claims in stinging irony against them. Yes, they will advance (in knowledge, thus referring to Gnostics?), but their advancement will be from bad to worse! The would-be false teachers who threaten to entice unsuspecting souls will themselves be enticed to evil along with their followers.

In the midst of stress caused by apparently successful teachers, the younger man is tempted to mimic these successful actions. In order to effectively fight against the threat of evil, should one be evil in return? The temptation to work as evil men do is sometimes an overwhelming temptation. Someone has said to beware when fighting a monster that we do not ourselves become the monster we are fighting. Paul's stance, while it may appear to be a weaker stance in the short run, is actually the stronger stance since it is firmly rooted in the very nature and character of God.

Up to this point the entire chapter has centered on the very real and apparently active threat to the Christian congregation by false teachers and deliberately evil individuals. Now Timothy is placed in sharp contrast to these people.

In verse 14, which begins *But as for you*, Timothy is to maintain his own integrity as a Christian by remembering what he has learned and known to be sufficient in the past through his family (his mother and grandmother, recall 1:5), from others (recall *many witnesses* mentioned in 2:2), and from Paul. He has learned through his own experience and through careful meditation on and study of the Scriptures.

Timothy Has Scripture (3:15-17)

In the Jewish tradition, children began learning Scripture at the age of five. The term *sacred writings* (used only here in the entire New Testament) means the

Hebrew Scriptures (Torah, Prophets, and Writings), or what Christians know as the Old Testament. Christian interpretation of the Scriptures understands the Old Testament to point toward salvation though Jesus Christ. By directing Timothy's attention to the long-cherished Scriptures, Paul may be hinting at the utter uselessness of the false teachers' preference for the myths and genealogies of extraneous tradition that were not written down but simply passed along by speaking. He may also be deriding the books and charms of people like the magician in Ephesus (Acts 19:19).

Recall the introductory observation that early in the process of collecting what became canon, Paul's own letters became a part of the Christian corpus (2 Peter 3:15).

The chapter concludes in verses 16-17 with a defense of the Scriptures as a means by which Timothy may successfully maintain his faith in the midst of trial. These two verses are frequently occasions of heated debate. Certainly Paul intended them to be a final statement of authority, thus equipping Timothy for the hard fight. In more recent times, however, they have become problematic for many Christians. What do they mean?

We must begin by assessing their original meaning. The Greek word for *scripture* is *graphe*. The term is used in one of two ways. First, Paul himself had found Scripture to be of immeasurable comfort (see Romans 15:4). The term describes Scripture as a whole (see Galatians 3:8, 22). Paul alludes to the well-known narrative of Elijah in his letter to the Romans (see Romans 11:2).

Occasionally, the term is used to describe a specific verse or reference, as in Matthew's gospel where Psalm 118:22-23 is cited (see Matthew 21:42). In John's gospel, Zechariah 12:10 is cited (John 19:37). The word for *inspired* takes its cue from the Genesis account of Creation. Recall that as God created the first human being, God breathed life into the created individual. The Greek means literally *breath given by God*.

We can see how Paul intends to correct the potential misleading of the false teachers whose teaching is not given by God (recall 1 Timothy 1:8-10).

The mention of *reproof,* that is, a combination of refutation with false teachers and a combatting of sin, gives further evidence of Paul's unshakable confidence in the power of the Scriptures that are deeply rooted in Israel's and the church's history. Reference to Scripture in this sense is a reference to an unassailable authority.

Correction in this context means a placing upright, putting people back on their feet in a moral sense. One gets the sense that the false teachers have disrupted any sort of moral equilibrium and balance. The Scriptures serve to restore moral balance.

Scriptures are to be used for *training in righteousness* (see Titus 2:11-14).

The density of Paul's argument is not regarding the specific language of inspiration or authority, though those facets are used advisedly. Rather, in verse 17 Paul points toward the result and purpose of Scripture, specifically that individuals may be equipped for what will inevitably be very difficult, demanding, and arduous undertakings in the Christian enterprise. In the original Greek, the reference is to a single man, that the *man . . . may be complete.* This may imply that Paul is thinking of a specific man, that is, Timothy (see 1 Timothy 6:11), or perhaps another Christian leader. But the truth of the insight is equally applicable to all Christians of any age.

Characteristic of the Pastoral Epistles is a concern for doing good, charitable works (recall 1 Timothy 2:10; 5:10; 2 Timothy 2:21; also see Titus 3:1).

§ § § § § § §

The Message of 2 Timothy 3

Chapter 3 presents to the younger minister, in no uncertain terms, the environment in which he will be carrying out his ministry. By no means can Timothy or anyone else in the congregation expect to give witness to the work of God through Christ without evoking an angry response. Paul summons the preacher to examine the hard facts of personal knowledge and experience that are supported by the tradition of the Scriptures.

What can we learn from this chapter?

§ The ways people act are symptoms of their separation from God.

§ Self-centered people will inevitably exhibit antisocial behavior.

§ Lonely and trapped people are prime subjects not only for Christian missionary activity but also for evil intent.

§ There is no authority with quite the same power as personal authority based on experience and hard-won moral victories.

§ When evil has its hour, the purposes of God will eventually carry the day.

§ The Scriptures are inspired by God.

§ The Bible points toward salvation through Christ.

§ The Bible gives a firm foundation to the spiritual lives of struggling people.

§ In the spirit of the letter, any argument about what inspiration means falls into the trap of arguing incessantly over a debate that no one can win.

§ The study of Scripture equips us for the tasks of ministry in a hostile environment which will resent any good, any creative, and any higher motive.

§ § § § § § §

2 Timothy 4

Introduction to This Chapter

An overview of the entire letter indicates that either Timothy has given ample reason for Paul to be concerned, or Paul has inferred from correspondence or other communication that the younger preacher is on the verge of conceding defeat to the stresses that abound in the Ephesian church. Earlier Timothy had been urged to *rekindle the gift* and *not be ashamed* of the gospel (1:6, 8, 13); *to be strong in the grace* of Christ (2:1-3, 8, 15); and to continue what he had seen and learned from firsthand experience (3:14). In this final chapter, Paul renews the theme that has been developed earlier in his final appeal to Timothy to preach the gospel.

Here is an outline of 2 Timothy 4.

I. A Final Appeal to Preach the Gospel (4:1-2)
II. Healthy and Unhealthy Religion (4:3-5)
III. An Approaching End (4:6-8)
IV. Personal Words (4:9-18)
V. Closing Salutations (4:19-21)
VI. A Benediction (4:22)

A Final Appeal to Preach the Gospel (4:1-2)

In 1 Timothy 5:21 Timothy had been similarly charged as in verse 1. However, here the instruction is intensified by the addition of God and Christ as witnesses to the apostle's statement.

In Peter's speech to Cornelius, the image of Christ as

judge is used (see Acts 10:42). First Peter 4:5 uses the same imagery. Paul's usage suggests two possibilities. Since Paul is near his own death (see verse 6), he may be suggesting that Timothy will be judged while he is alive, and Paul when he is dead. Or he may be suggesting that Christ is the judge of both of them whether alive or dead. In either interpretation, the point is that Christ is judge and Timothy's ministry will be duly examined and Timothy held accountable.

The term for *appearing* is *epiphany* (recall 1 Timothy 6:14; see Titus 2:13).

The mention of the *kingdom* summons Timothy and the church to the higher goal of God's intention and method as well as the sovereignty of Christ.

Preach the word in verse 2 reminds the preacher of his first responsibility. The verb *preach* carries with it the connotation of standing up and challenging both Christian and false teacher alike with the gospel.

Be urgent in season and out of season suggests two possibilities. First, the apostle knows that in the immediate stress of conflict or challenge, the preacher will not have time to properly reflect and prepare all of his messages and/or responses. Therefore, the minister will be able to draw only on what he has internalized. In other words, a minister cannot wait until the crisis is at hand before beginning preparations in earnest. Perhaps Paul is reflecting on the athlete's experience. He knows that when the competition begins, it is too late to begin thinking about the sort of preparation that should have been done in order to be competitive. Therefore, the minister must be steadily at the disciplines of preparation.

A second possibility emerges. The younger preacher may be inclined to wait until his listeners are ready to receive his gospel message. Paul had already had one instance in which a colleague had decided not to pursue a missionary journey (see 1 Corinthians 16:12). In

Timothy's case, the minister is told to preach urgently whether the congregation seems to be urgent or not. In both interpretations, the counsel suggests a constant need for diligence in preparation and preaching the word. One thing is certain. If the preacher does not consider the word to be urgent both in the crisis and in ordinary time, neither will the congregation.

In addition to preaching, the minister's responsibility includes diligent pastoral oversight through convincing, admonishing, and exhorting. Paul is well aware of the demands of pastoral oversight (see 1 Corinthians 5:1-2). The offending individuals should be put out of the fellowship. In another circumstance, an offender is to be overwhelmed with love (2 Corinthians 2:7-8).

Healthy and Unhealthy Religion (4:3-5)

Part of the stress of the time (recall 3:1) is that some members of the congregation may not have as much patience with their minister who will not tell them what they want to hear. Indeed, some members will have *tingling ears* and will tolerate only those doctrines and preaching that they want to hear. These folks will find another preacher, or would-be preacher, who preaches their gospel. Doubtless they can find a preacher who is blithely for them all the time.

The tragic irony is that the preachers who say only what people want to hear are ultimately not for their people. The people who seek only a comfortable and non-threatening message may be pursuing their own ruin by following what is actually unhealthy religion (recall 1 Timothy 1:4).

What is the Christian minister to do in this circumstance? Timothy, and other ministers of the gospel, should remain resolutely disciplined and clearheaded. Under no circumstances should the Christian minister flinch from suffering. In all circumstances the minister should do the work of an evangelist.

An Approaching End (4:6-8)

Timothy is to fulfill his ministry to the best that he knows, because Paul can no longer exercise his ministry since he is near the end of his own journey.

The word *sacrifice* means literally poured out on the altar. (See also Philippians 2:17.) The image comes from the Jewish tradition of pouring as part of the daily offerings at the Temple. Instructions are given in the Book of Exodus (see Exodus 29:40).

The metaphor changes from the Temple sacrifice to either the sea and a vessel's departure or soldiers who are about to begin a campaign. In another letter, Paul uses the term *depart* for death (see Philippians 1:23).

Some scholars suggest that this verse, with its images of departure and death, accounts in part for the arrangement of the letters. First Timothy is longer, but Second Timothy contains this poignant departure scene.

The thought of impending death causes reflection by the old apostle in verse 7. Looking back over the long course of events since his dramatic conversion years earlier, Paul summarizes his life: *I have fought the good fight*. As he has earlier (recall 1 Timothy 6:12), Paul employs a metaphor from athletic competition. The fight here does not indicate a military metaphor, especially since the image continues in the next verse with the awarding of a laurel wreath to the victors.

Some readers may hear a certain arrogance in Paul's claim. However, this would be a misreading. Paul is calling attention to the high calling of ministry. Granted, throughout the letters thus far Paul has summoned the younger preacher to emulate the highest motives and most compassionate and courageous actions. But Paul does not seem to be drawing attention to his own victory, but rather is pointing toward the effort itself.

Finishing the race sounds like a mixed metaphor. What is important is that Paul continues with the athletic imagery.

In the Greek, the phrase *I have kept the faith* (RSV) (recall 1 Timothy 6:20; 2 Timothy 1:12, 14) can also be translated, *I have been loyal to the trust.* The trust refers not only to the Christian faith but also to the trust that God has placed in him. Throughout his ministry, in even the worst circumstances, Paul remained loyal to the higher calling and to God, who summoned him to the higher calling.

The athletic image continues through to the victory stand in verse 8. Paul anticipates receiving his reward. Not only did Greeks award garlands to victors, but in Jewish tradition wreaths of flowers or leaves were worn during celebrations. Note how Paul is constantly alluding to the rich tradition of Judaism while at the same time drawing illustrations from the common daily experience of the young preacher.

Laid up (literally "is in store") *for me* is a technical term that was used in giving rewards for service.

What is the *crown of righteousness* (literally the garland of righteousness) to which Paul looks? Two possible interpretations can be made. He may be alluding to the crown of life (see James 1:12 for a similar reference). Or the crown may refer to the appropriate reward for any who have lived an upright and righteous life (recall 3:16).

Some interpreters question the overt claim that Christ himself will reward Paul, because Paul seems to be drawing too much attention to himself and his own achievements. However, the apostle continues by saying that the reward is not uniquely his. Indeed, the same reward, presumably from the same returning Christ, is available to all Christians. Paul considers himself to be one of the people.

Christians await the return of Christ (see Philippians 3:20). In his closing benediction to the Corinthians, Paul utters the Christian hope, *Our Lord, come!* In the final words of Revelation, the Christian hope is similarly expressed (Revelation 22:20).

Personal Words (4:9-18)

Through a series of intensely personal requests and remarks, Paul gives a brief description of his present circumstances. Paul is utterly isolated due to a number of developments.

Demas, which may be a shortened form of the name *Demetrius*, has deserted him. He is listed as a fellow worker in Philemon 24, and in Colossians 4:14 he is listed along with Luke. The specific reason that Demas left Paul is not given. Many interpreters suggest apostasy. However, the text reads *in love with this present world*. Perhaps the stress of ministry in a hostile environment became too much and Demas simply could not stand the isolation or suffering. He may have gone to another city, perhaps Thessalonica, to continue his work under more amenable circumstances.

Crescens, about whom we know nothing, may have gone to Gaul (France), thus indicating an expanding Christian missionary field.

Titus has gone to Dalmatia. Dalmatia includes the southern part of the province of Illyricum (see Romans 15:19) and territory along the western shore of the Adriatic (modern day Yugoslavia).

Of the many people who used to be with him, only Luke, who had been with him earlier, remains.

Paul's relationship with Mark has been a stormy one. In Acts Paul refuses to take Mark along on the subsequent journey since Mark had not stayed with him in an earlier crisis in Pamphylia (see Acts 15:38-39). Over the course of years, however, the rupture did not remain permanent. Mark became one of Paul's companions (see Colossians 4:10). In the context of Paul's final words to Timothy, Mark appears to be a personal assistant or an assistant in ministry.

Tychicus is an Asian-born man who became an assistant to and companion with Paul on the final missionary journey. His name appears in the list of persons accompanying Paul as he set sail for Syria (see Acts 20:4). He is the man who carried Paul's letters to both the Colossians (Colossians 4:7-8) and the Ephesians (Ephesians 6:21-22). One further possibility exists. Paul could have sent Tychicus to Ephesus to be Timothy's assistant, though we have no way of verifying this.

Following the list of names, Paul gives specific instructions in verse 13. He needs his *cloak* (a winter outer garment worn over other clothing), his *books*, and his *parchments*.

Paul had been to Troas many times (Acts 16:8; 20:6; 2 Corinthians 2:12).

About Carpus we know nothing. He is named only here in the New Testament.

Books and *parchments* offer interesting insights into Paul's own study and writing. The books are papyrus rolls containing already written material, in all likelihood some Scriptures that are particularly important to Paul. Parchment is a single piece of skin or vellum that could be used any number of times for writing. The request therefore could easily have been a request for his own personal notebooks or sheaves of loose sheets on which he has been keeping notes, study references (probably proof texts from the Old Testament), or special correspondence not yet completed.

In verses 14-16 Alexander's name is listed. Why had his name not been included in the earlier listing of both high reputation and lower reputation men? Is this the same Alexander who had been pressed into emergency service in Ephesus earlier in Paul's ministry (Acts 19:33)? He may also be the Alexander mentioned in 1 Timothy 1:20. And what were the specific actions of this man against Paul? He may have been a witness against the apostle at his trial. Citing an ancient Hebrew hope (Psalm 28:4), Paul has utter confidence that God will have the final word. To the Romans Paul had expressed similar trust in God (Romans 12:19). Timothy is to stay clear of Alexander.

Paul refers to his *first defense* in verse 16. This may mean that he had been tried in an earlier trial and acquitted. Acts 28 does suggest that he has relative freedom, during which time he is able to continue his missionary preaching. The reference may be to an interim time between first hearing and actual trial. Evidently the Roman congregation is unable to muster sufficient courage to stand with Paul in his trial. But here Paul seems to understand the stress. They are not condemned. Perhaps the time is simply not right for a public display of solidarity in the face of a hostile Roman government.

In verse 17, since Paul has no visible support from fellow Christians, he does find the presence of God to be sufficient. Note how the apostle is able to take even the most distressing circumstance and interpret it to show the sufficiency of God. Surely the argument cannot be lost on Timothy, who also has to trust God's sufficiency in the Ephesian church. Note that throughout his ministry Paul stresses the universal implications of the gospel. He still stresses the advancement of the gospel to the Gentiles.

Giving further evidence of God's providential care, Paul is rescued. The phrase *rescued from the lion's mouth* is taken from Psalms 17:12; 35:17; Daniel 6:16-23. The image is of rescue, but does not necessarily refer to a Roman emperor (that is, Nero), or to the devil.

In verse 18 Paul continues to build the images of rescue through what may be a quotation from the Lord's prayer (Matthew 6:13). Here Paul seems less concerned about physical rescue form the Roman authorities than he is about his own spiritual and moral state.

The *heavenly kingdom* is both a present promise and a future hope (see 1 Corinthians 15:50).

The reference to the eternal kingdom of God prompts a doxology that is exactly the same as Galatians 1:5. Paul frequently uses doxologies in his letters; see Romans 9:5; 11:36; Ephesians 3:21; Philippians 4:20. Earlier in First Timothy Paul had included a doxology (1:17).

FIRST TIMOTHY THROUGH PHILEMON

Closing Salutations (4:19-21)

The letter concludes with further final greetings to cherished friends and acquaintances.

Prisca is a variation of the name *Priscilla*. She, along with Aquila, is mentioned six times in the New Testament. They served faithfully in Corinth (Acts 18:2). They had to leave Rome due to an edict forbidding Jews from the city. They had accompanied Paul to Ephesus (Acts 18:19). In his letter to the Romans, Paul identifies them as accompanying him in that city (Romans 16:3).

The household of Onesiphorus is mentioned, though he himself is assumed to be dead (recall 1:16).

Verse 20 states that Erastus had stayed behind in Corinth. In Romans 16:23 Erastus is listed as the treasurer. In Acts 19:22 Paul sends Erastus with Timothy to Macedonia. Presumably this means the same man; however, his identity is uncertain.

Trophimus, a former associate (Acts 20:4; 21:29), had stayed in Miletus due to sickness.

Four names are written in Latin: *Eubulus*, *Prudens*, *Linus*, and *Claudia*. Only one of the names can be identified. Linus succeeded Peter as Bishop of Rome.

A Benediction (4:22)

The final verse is similar to Galatians 6:18 and Philemon 25. Not readily apparent in the English translation is the use of plural *you*. Paul knew that the letter would not only be read in private by the younger minister, it would also be read aloud to the congregation in the course of public worship (recall 1 Timothy 6:21). The message of encouragement and the sufficiency of God for all circumstances is not restricted to one or two of Paul's closest associates; it is also for the entire church.

§ § § § § § §

The Message of 2 Timothy 4

In this chapter we have heard the intensely personal voice of Paul giving witness to the strength that he has received from God when all those around him had either failed or been unavailable for support. The letter therefore concludes with incontrovertible evidence of the sufficiency of God for Timothy and the entire church.

What else can we learn from this chapter?

§ The preacher's task is one of eternal weight and dimension.

§ A person cannot wait for public appeal for the gospel; there is an urgency to the gospel that cares not a bit about the desires of people.

§ In every age there will be people who want a teacher or preacher who says what is comfortable and/or novel.

§ The Christian preacher and teacher knows of the eternal truth of God and will therefore not be swayed by temporary whims and fads in thinking.

§ The Christian life requires a lifetime to complete.

§ Christians have an eternal hope, hope of the kingdom of God.

§ Study and writing are authentic and legitimate disciplines for preachers, teachers, and other Christians.

§ God's strength will be sufficient for every need.

§ God will protect our going out and our coming in from this time forth and forevermore.

§ The final word is a blessing word; a distinctively Christian act is the power to bless.

§ § § § § § §

Titus 1

Introduction to This Chapter

Unlike Timothy, Titus is not mentioned in the Book of Acts at all. He is mentioned frequently in Paul's second letter to the Corinthians and Galatians. A Gentile (see Galatians 2:3), he became one of Paul's fellow workers. After his conversion, Paul went to Jerusalem accompanied by Barnabas and Titus (Galatians 2:1-10). When Paul heard of the Corinthian church's refusal to heed his authority, Paul sent Titus to ascertain the conditions of the church. Paul would follow later by a prescribed route.

However, Titus was not at the appointed meeting place, Troas (2 Corinthians 2:13). They did meet later in Macedonia (2 Corinthians 7:6). The report Titus brought encouraged Paul, as the hostility that had been reported was no longer apparent. Indeed, the church seemed prepared to heed his authority once again (2 Corinthians 7:9, 13-14). Paul sent Titus back to Corinth to continue the work that had started so auspiciously earlier (2 Corinthians 8:6). The congregation's response to Titus would give evidence of their true Christian character and grace, especially through the contribution that was being collected for the saints in Jerusalem.

Paul had been in Crete on a missionary journey and is now elsewhere (Titus 1:5). Accurate dating of the letter is very difficult. Christian congregations are assumed to be in existence on Crete, since Paul refers to entire families (1:11). In fact, there seem to be many churches in many different cities on the island. Titus's responsibility is to complete the task of organizing these new congregations.

The letter's purpose is similar to the purpose of the letters to Timothy, to elevate the quality of character to Christian standards. We have seen in the earlier epistles that the emphasis is on the character of the teachers and their teaching. In Titus the emphasis is on the character of the people being taught. By any measure, Crete is a difficult appointment. Titus would have to compete with a tradition of competition between cities on the island, the fact that the island had been a center for piracy in the Mediterranean, and had been subdued by the Romans, much to the Cretans' dislike. Only since 67 B.C. had the area been a Roman province.

Here is an outline of Titus 1.

I. Greeting (1:1-4)
II. Commands to Titus (1:5-16)
   A. Regarding ministry and church officials (1:5-9)
   B. A word about opponents (1:10-16)

Greeting (1:1-4)

The opening address is much longer than either of the introductory addresses of First or Second Timothy. The introduction is comparable to Romans 1:1-7 and Galatians 1:1-5, and it is different in tone from the other Pastorals. In this introduction Paul speaks to Titus as a father speaking to a son. The introduction also includes instructions from the apostle to the delegate to another church.

The stress is on duty rather than authority. In fact, little is mentioned regarding Paul's authority.

The message that Titus is to communicate is deeply rooted in the past, yet it looks forward with great anticipation to the future. In the tension between past and future the Christian is to live a godly life.

Only here in verse 1 does Paul use the expression *servant of God.* Elsewhere Paul employs the term *servant of*

Jesus Christ (Romans 1:1; Philippians 1:1) and *the Lord's servant* (2 Timothy 2:24). The phrase is used in the Old Testament for such figures as Moses, prophets (Daniel 9:10-11), and even non-Israelites whom God uses (Isaiah 45:1, 5). Among the best-known servant passages are the servant songs in Isaiah 42:1-4; 49:1-6; 50:4-9; 52:13–53:12.

In addition to the identity as *servant*, the authority of *apostle* is added. Apostle carries with it a stronger sense of authority. One further interpretation is that Paul is carrying out an assignment by God as an apostle with the authority of Jesus Christ.

Knowledge, truth, and *accord* are specific terms which reveal a relatively sophisticated schema by which the Christian faith is understood and measured. Two possibilities emerge. First, Paul may be suggesting that he has been chosen in accordance with the standards of the faith. More likely, he is framing the work of ministry, especially preaching and teaching, in the context of an accepted standard.

Many different terms are used to describe God's people, that is, the church. The term *God's elect* evokes the tradition of God's chosen people (Isaiah 43:20-21; 65:9). Only Paul uses the term in the New Testament (Romans 8:33; Colossians 3:12). The implication is quite clear. God chooses the church, not the reverse.

In the other Pastoral Letters, knowledge (*gnosis*) as espoused by the false teachers is condemned as worthless and empty-headed. Paul does not, however, condemn all knowledge out of hand. Critical discernment is necessary.

The *truth* (recall 1 Timothy 2:4; 2 Timothy 2:25; 3:7) means the Christian faith. The truth does not exist in a vacuum. Instead, the truth of the Christian faith is directly related to godliness (1 Timothy 6:3) which in turn points toward eternal life.

The task of the apostle/preacher in verse 2 is to build the hope of people, thus giving them a context of eternity for their faith and moral character.

Their hope is not a vacant illusion. To the contrary, their hope is grounded in God, who does not lie (Romans 3:3-4), but has promised life through all eternity (Ephesians 2:4-6). In Acts 3:18 Peter preaches, *what God foretold by the mouth of all the prophets, that his Christ should suffer.*

In verse 3, God's timing remains a mystery; no human being can determine when God will act. In Greek the word for the right moment is *kairos* (Galatians 4:4). John the Baptist's preaching emphasizes God's good timing (see Mark 1:15). Incarnation means much more than simply the narrative and events surrounding the birth of the baby Jesus. Incarnation means the entirety of Jesus' birth, life, ministry, death, and resurrection.

However, God is manifested not only through the person of Jesus but also through preaching—not only Paul's preaching, but all preaching which is in accord with the apostolic tradition of proclamation. Viewed in this perspective, preaching is a sacrament rather than mere exhortation or admonition. Paul is a preacher due to God's own election and commission. This affirmation may be in response to false teachers who are trying to usurp authority in the church.

For the term *God our Savior* recall 1 Timothy 1:1.

After the long introduction, Titus is finally addressed in verse 4. Paul holds the younger preacher in high regard. At one point Paul refers to Titus as his *brother* (2 Corinthians 2:13). Titus had more than adequately served the apostle as a fellow worker in the Corinthian church (2 Corinthians 8:23). Paul characterizes him as acting in the same spirit as Paul himself (2 Corinthians 12:18). Titus is indeed *a true child in a common faith* whose life is to be a *model* (2:7) for others to follow.

Throughout the Book of Acts and Paul's ministry, the universal implications and direction of the gospel are stressed. Here a variation on the theme occurs. The *common faith* means a common faith between Jew and

Gentile. Jude 3 contains a similar affirmation.

Grace and *peace* occur without the addition of mercy as in 1 Timothy 1:2; 2 Timothy 1:2.

God is identified as Father through whom Paul is related to Titus.

Note the unusual construction of placing Jesus Christ and God in the same phrase, on the same plane, thus equally important in the overall purpose of salvation.

Regarding Ministry and Church Officials (1:5-9)

At verse 5 the instructions to Titus begin. The instructions are very similar to the instructions given in 1 Timothy 3:1-7. The main qualifications of elders/presbyters are the same. However, 1 Timothy reflects a Christian community that is older and better organized than the congregations to which Titus must minister. Note that the Timothy list includes verification of character by other witnesses and excludes individuals who have only recently been converted. Furthermore, the Timothy list includes regulations regarding deacons and deaconesses as well. No such category exists in Titus's instructions. Ordination is assumed but not described.

Titus has the authority to organize the Christian congregations. In Timothy elders are already working in the church. On Crete Titus will have to start from the beginning by appointing elders. Correspondingly, the qualifications for elders are limited to personal moral standards as verified through family life. Delegation of authority is not unusual. In Acts responsibilities are delegated to selected individuals. The selection of deacons in Acts 6:1-6 gives a picture of such delegation (see also Acts 14:21-23).

Though Titus has the authority and freedom to select and appoint elders, each of the elders must be someone of whom Paul himself would approve. Perhaps Paul is anticipating conflict with Cretans as he has encountered conflict with Ephesians (recall 2 Timothy 4:14).

The qualifications for bishop/elder (the terms are interchangeable) in verse 6 parallel the qualifications listed in 1 Timothy 3:2-7. The closeness of the parallel prompts some scholars to suggest that Titus 1:7-9 is an inserted piece.

As with the Ephesian congregation, Paul begins with his concern about the elder's family and the possible difficulties that could result from a poorly managed family. The elder must be above reproach. He must be married to one wife, that is, married only once. His children must themselves be Christian believers. The children must not bring criticism on the church because they act like the proverbial prodigal son and bring ruin upon themselves and, by implication, upon the reputation of the church. Presumably this implies financial foolishness, since the verb used is the same verb as in Luke 15:13 where the meaning suggests financial ruin. Nor should they be insubordinate (see 1 Timothy 3:4), either within the confines of the home or in public through challenging civic officials.

Following the characterization of the elder and his family, a negative list of qualifications appears in verse 7. Almost in passing Paul indicates the reason for avoiding negative action: The elder is a *steward* of *God* over the household of God. Note the recurrent theme of the household.

Five negative qualifications are: (1) The elder should not be self-willed and obstinate. He cannot arrogantly hold to his own opinion without regard for others. (2) He should not be quick-tempered since pastoral work regularly requires great patience both with individuals and with organizational structures. (3) He should not be overly dependent upon wine. Recall that earlier Paul had counseled Timothy to drink a little wine occasionally. (4) An elder must not be violent with his congregation. Presumably this means physical violence. We may well add emotional violence, since in his second letter to the

Corinthians Paul mentions the possibility of both physical and emotional abuse (2 Corinthians 11:20). (5) An elder must not be greedy for personal monetary gain. The central point is that if the elder places his own gain ahead of the integrity of the gospel, he may fall into the habit of changing his preaching so that it is more to the liking of the congregation/audience (recall the caution of 1 Timothy 6:5). Such behavior is suggested in verse 11. Selfish motivation may find elders seizing for themselves offerings that are intended for others. To the Corinthians Paul defended himself against similar inferences (2 Corinthians 11:17). A final possibility exists. The selfishly motivated elder may be willing to enter into trades or business that would discredit the church. Paul himself set a high example (see Acts 20:33-34).

A list of Christian virtues follows in verse 8 (note the parallel with 2 Timothy 3:2): (1) *hospitable* first out of love for others and secondly to traveling Christian missionaries or evangelists; (2) a *lover of goodness*, wherever he finds it (Paul counsels the Philippians similarly in 4:8); (3) *upright*, just; (4) *holy* in the sense of being authentically pious and devout; (5) *master of himself*, self-disciplined and sensible, a gift of the Spirit (Galatians 5:23).

Verse 9 states that in addition to personal characteristics, an elder must also hold firmly to the faith for his own sake and for the sake of the congregation to which he is appointed. The temptation to adapt doctrinal statements to what men and women want to hear is ongoing. The doctrinal standard to which elders must cling is nothing less than the apostolic tradition that the apostle Paul himself preached. The verse implies an already-existing written codification of some kind of doctrine (Romans 16:17). Similar evidence exists in the letters to Timothy: 1 Timothy 6:20; 2 Timothy 1:13; 2:2.

A Word About Opponents (1:10-16)

The previous verses presented the personal and

doctrinal qualifications of any would-be elder. Now in verse 10 Paul gives the reasons for these demands. The false teachers are an insubordinate lot with the disturbing habit of challenging Christian authorities. The teachers about whom Paul speaks are not pagans. They are themselves Christians (verse 16) from predominantly Jewish background (verse 10). Evidently some of these teachers want to dwell on Jewish legends regarding the patriarchs and in the process add to the Christian practice duties that have no real divine authority (verse 15; also 3:9). Another difficulty is that the false teachers are not foreigners. They are Cretans themselves. Thus they will have a certain authority among their own people. In fact, the false teachers will be easily able to attract the more gullible of the native population.

The circumcision party has been a difficult sect of the Christian movement from the outset. This group posed a great threat to the missionary enterprise during the Jerusalem conference (Acts 15:1-29). The Galatian church found itself nearly split over the expectations demanded by the conservative, formerly Jewish, Christian circumcision party.

Paul characterizes these people as vain talkers (translated *empty talkers* in the RSV). The word vain/empty is a favorite word in Jewish tradition, and is used especially against pagan idol worship. Therefore, Paul is using the term with great sarcastic irony. The teaching of the false teachers is no higher than the teaching of the surrounding culture.

In unequivocal terms in verse 11 Paul demands that these false teachers be silenced. The verb used is actually *muzzled*, much like an animal would be muzzled. The field of the false teachers' work is precisely the place where the Christian movement has had remarkable success: the home, where careful guidance and training occur as in no other setting.

Worse yet is the motive for the false teachers' activity:

FIRST TIMOTHY THROUGH PHILEMON

base gain. They hope to receive personal gifts from their hearers (1 Timothy 5:17-18; 6:5).

Paul's characterizations are accurate; they are corroborated by the witness of another Cretan. Some commentators wonder why Paul would be so blunt with his assertions. Surely he could have known that this letter would be read aloud, within the hearing of a Cretan audience. Perhaps Paul is relying upon the depth of Christian conviction and identity to offset any feeling of national or native pride.

The word translated *testimony* (RSV) stems from the same word as *martyr* in the Greek language.

Only short segments of the false teachings are given in verse 14; presumably Titus and his hearers would have been familiar with the problem and therefore would not have needed further explanation.

The false teachers' doctrines include Jewish fables and myths (recall 1 Timothy 1:4), and also the tradition of the elders (Mark 7:3-4, 8).

Against the ascetic false teachers, Paul posits his own perspective in what may be a proverbial saying in verse 15. The notion has its origins in Hebrew thought in Haggai 2:12-14. Then he makes the further point that the false teachers have utterly lost the capacity for moral and spiritual discernment; their judgment is thoroughly perverted. They cannot tell the difference between good and bad anymore (see 1 Timothy 4:2; 6:5; 2 Timothy 3:8).

In verse 16, evidence of the spiritual wrecks that the false teachers have made of their lives comes at the point of inconsistency between what they say and what they do. The Gnostics claimed a higher, more sophisticated knowledge. With their supposed intellectual superiority they acted above others. Paul punctures their false superiority with the scathing indictment that behavior is the manifestation of true character. In the New Testament many voices reiterate this same insight (James 2:14-17).

§ § § § § § §

The Message of Titus 1

Titus has been left in an inhospitable place to do a very difficult task. He is to appoint elders who themselves need to aspire to the highest Christian goals and motives, who will assist in correcting the deplorable moral and spiritual conditions in Crete. Against Titus's efforts will be arrayed an intimidating collection of people who consider themselves intellectually and spiritually superior to the paltry efforts of the Christian minister.

However, Paul refuses to allow the circumstances to defeat the Christian missionary enterprise. Instead, Paul takes the circumstances as part of the definition of what the minister's work is.

What else can we learn from this chapter?

§ No one can be called to a calling higher than leading the people of God to the highest possible attainment of character.

§ The motive for excellent moral and spiritual character is eternal life.

§ Christian ministers lead by moral example as well as by doctrinal teaching and pulpit eloquence.

§ People will be willing to listen to one of their own before listening to the discerning outsider.

§ Uncomfortable as it is, ministers can be identified by bad example as well as by good example.

§ Beware of premature dependence upon half a truth.

§ Consciences can become incapable of discerning right from wrong; good from bad; healthy from unhealthy religion.

§ Our actions speak at least as loudly as our words.

§ § § § § § §

Titus 2

Introduction to This Chapter

Set in the context of how the preacher should deal with various elements in the congregation—men, women, and slaves—three themes are developed in Titus 2. The chapter is a recapitulation of and an enlargement upon the directives given in Titus 1. The importance of the family is again emphasized. Throughout the chapter Paul shows the relationship between God's intention and human actions or motives.

One of Paul's recurrent themes is the family (see Ephesians 5:22–6:9; Colossians 3:18–4:1). The family has already been discussed in the Pastorals, especially in 1 Timothy 5:1–6:2. Concern for the family and groups within the church is also expressed in 1 Peter 2:18–3:7, which emphasizes the same theme through an address to slaves (verse 18), wives, and husbands (3:1, 7).

The term *in order that* (in the Greek language) occurs six times in this single chapter (verses 4, 5, 8, 10, 12, 14). In each instance the linkage is between God's purpose and human action or attitude. The usage is not apparent in the English translations. Therefore, for the purposes of illustration, a literal translation follows:

Verse 4 (*in order that they may train*), linking God's intention that the generations can cooperate.

Verse 5 (*in order that/lest the word of God be blasphemed*), linking God's intention with the younger generation's attitude and action.

Verse 8 (*in order that the opponents can be shamed*), linking God's purpose with the preacher's action.

Verse 10 (*in order that the teaching of the Savior might adorn all*), even teaching by slaves!

Verse 12 (*in order that we might live*), linking incarnation with how we live.

Verse 14 (*in order that we might live free from the power of death*), linking God's promise with human moral effort.

Here is an outline of Chapter 2.

I. Dealing With Older Men (2:1-2)
II. Dealing With Older Women (2:3-5)
III. Dealing With Younger Men (2:6-8)
IV. Dealing With Slaves (2:9-10)
V. What God Expects From All Christians (2:11-15)

Dealing With Older Men (2:1-2)

Recall that Chapter 1 concludes with a ringing denouncement of teachers who make the pretense of knowing God but whose actions betray their falseness. Titus is to be remarkably different from them: *But as for you . . . .*

Correct behavior depends upon correct belief, that is, *sound doctrine* (recall 1:9; also 1 Timothy 1:10).

The groupings begin in verse 2 with the oldest members of the church. In the Greek language the term used is the same term that is translated *elder*, meaning an official leader of the church. However, in this context, the word means simply *elders*. The elders are described as *temperate, serious*, and *sensible*.

The word *temperate* carries two possible connotations. The first is the notion of sobriety, that the older men should be moderate in their drinking habits. The other alternative is that they should be temperate and dignified in their judgments (recall 1 Timothy 3:2). Since the word *grave* (*serious*) follows, it seems that the latter interpretation is more accurate.

Serious and *sensible* suggest the images of wise older

men who are to live lives of deliberate counsel in the community. These characteristics are similarly identified in 1 Timothy (2:2; 3:2, 8).

The second set of descriptions takes its cue from those who are *sound* or perhaps healthy in their religion. The elders are to be *sound in their faith, in love, and in steadfastness* or endurance. This triple description is also found in 1 Timothy 6:11 and 2 Timothy 3:10, as well as 1 Thessalonians 1:3.

What is the point of this threefold expectation? First, the initial description is in a sense little more than a repetition of the highest ethical impulse within the surrounding pagan culture. That is, older men are supposed to be the wise ones who will by their nature be temperate and serious. Therefore, the second listing adds a specifically Christian dimension to the instructions given first.

Second, Paul recognizes the liability of a strength. A strength can easily become a weakness. Therefore, he links the essential ethics with the larger motive of Christian faith. Jesus recognized the possibility that even the impulse to the higher calling may be lost (Matthew 24:12). In Titus's circumstances, where persecution is a very real possibility (2:8), he needs a foundation deeper than sheer human will or moral grit.

The word *love* is *agape*, which means the kind of love that God expresses toward the creation. Unlike the weak and oversentimental notion of love that modern persons have, *agape* is a resolute, deeply committed, long-suffering love that will not be easily deterred.

Why does the list conclude with steadfastness? Since steadfastness carries with it the connotation of endurance, Paul may be alluding to the actual as well as impending stresses within which Titus will have to minister on Crete. In addition, the word suggests something other than a callous and indifferent endurance similar to what the Stoics demanded.

Dealing With Older Women (2:3-5)

Older women in the congregation are charged with attitudes and behavior similar to those of the men, with the addition of being *reverent* in their demeanor and deportment as people would be if they were involved in sacred duties (recall 1 Timothy 2:10). They should not be gossipers or slanderers (1 Timothy 3:11).

The instructions for older women continue with the positive role that the women have. They are to *teach what is good*, if not through an official teaching capacity, then through moral example.

A third category or class of people is addressed in verse 4, the younger women of the church. Through the older women's teaching and moral example, the younger women will learn to love *their husbands and children*. Loving husband and children are virtues that were often noted in funeral inscriptions.

Presumably the model of the older women continues in verse 5. *Sensible* and *chaste*, or pure, address the need for a high standard with respect to sexual conduct.

The admonition to be *kind* adds a new element to domestic or family life. Specifically, slaves and servants are to be treated benevolently. Elsewhere instructions are given to Christian slaves (1 Peter 2:18).

The final instruction may strike a sensitive nerve in modern readers. Few people today read unhesitatingly that wives should be submissive to their husbands. For Paul the admonition is quite usual. To the Corinthians he had written that women should be silent in church (1 Corinthians 14:35). To the Colossians he gives the instructions, *Wives, be subject to your husbands, as is fitting in the Lord* (3:18). Similar counsel appears in Ephesians 5:22. We cannot condemn Paul's words as wrong or misled. He is writing within the context of a first and second century cultural milieu, taking as part of his cue his Jewish tradition. He could hardly ignore the predominant cultural norms.

The key to understanding this instruction follows. In part, the instruction may stem from the propensity of some women to feel the necessity of leaving their homes and families in order to enter into the religious life. Paul sets the family within the sphere of authentic and valid religious life.

Paul is concerned that some individuals are taking advantage of the Christian faith with its new emphasis on freedom. Such misappropriation of the faith threatens to unravel the fabric of society and culture. Behavior of this sort will inevitably bring scorn (or worse) upon the minority Christian movement. Recall 1 Timothy 3:7 where he emphasizes the reputation of the church. He simply does not want the new movement to open itself up for either scorn or scandal.

This verse and others like it pose particularly difficult questions. What is the role of the Christian church in society? The people of God must aspire to the higher calling and an identity that is significantly different from surrounding culture. We may be no closer than Paul was to resolving the conflicting claims of culture or faith, but at least we can begin by recognizing that the people of God will always live with the tension between culture and faith: identity as human in society and identity as a unique person of God.

Dealing With Younger Men (2:6-8)

The third category of persons to whom Paul addresses instructions is the younger men of the congregation. The younger men are to live chastely or purely, that is, exercising self-control (recall 1 Timothy 2:9 where women are supposed to adorn themselves modestly and sensibly) in all aspects of life.

Titus is addressed in verse 7, *show yourself*, serving to focus the behavior in one man's model (recall 1 Timothy 4:12).

Reflected in Paul's image of the good Christian

teacher/preacher is the negative image in verse 8 of the pagan who criticizes from the outside (2:5, 10; also 1 Timothy 5:14 and 1 Peter 2:12-15) as well as the possible critic from the inside (2 Timothy 2:25).

In short, Paul continues stressing the absolute need to monitor the content of preaching as well as the style or manner in which the preacher lives, always looking for an essential integrity.

Dealing With Slaves (2:9-10)

Slaves are the final group addressed. Again, as with the earlier admonition to wives, this verse may be a problem for modern readers. How could Paul speak to slaves without an accompanying moral outrage? Slavery was at that time in Christian history a fact of life. Here Paul implies that slaves, like all other Christians, have a moral responsibility and spiritual life. The charge is similar to the one made in 1 Timothy 6:1. Paul assumes slavery as a fact of life in other correspondence as well (see, for example, 1 Corinthians 7:21).

Slaves are to be obedient to masters in all respects. How can slaves live up to this high standard? They must consider themselves Christian human beings before they think of themselves as enslaved. Only then can slaves do their work without resorting to cheating or answering back in an attempt to preserve their pride and dignity. Doing the required work well is itself an expression of faithfulness to the gospel.

Note that Paul concludes the charge to slaves by focusing attention not on the servitude of people but on the gospel.

God our Savior is used earlier in 1 Timothy 1:1.

What God Expects From All Christians (2:11-15)

With no further explanation, the preceding charges sound like little more than moralisms: *You should do.* Therefore, verses 11-14 supply the theological undergirding and motivation for the higher calling to which each of the categories of people is called.

The moral life is set within the context of another life: the life of Jesus. Indeed, the grace of God would be little more than a notion, an idea, without a life that exhibits what this notion looks like in practice. The grace of God has appeared, been made manifest, through a real person who has known what it means to be fully human and fully alive in the context of real history working with real people.

The word used for *appeared* is *epiphany*. The word has two meanings. One meaning is the coming of light into darkness, as dawn gradually emerges from the darkness of night. Another is the sudden appearance through divine intervention. In Genesis just such an appearance occurs. Jacob is able to travel safely from Shechem to Mamre because God intervenes as a terror among the pursuing forces (Genesis 35:5).

In this context, the implication is that God intervened on behalf of all humankind through Jesus.

The coming of Christ in human form is called the *incarnation*. Frequently the incarnation is restricted to the celebration of the actual birth during the Christmas season. But the incarnation means much more than birth. In the New Testament, the incarnation implies the entirety of Jesus' life: birth, ministry, life, death, and resurrection. Therefore, this verse is an allusion to the entire life of Jesus, not just his birth.

The purpose of the incarnation is the salvation of all humankind. Now we can see the importance of the listings earlier in the chapter. Paul has suggested that all, regardless of age or station, have equal access to God's salvation. By implication Paul points toward the rest of pagan culture as well (verses 5, 8, 10). Certainly Paul's work as recalled in Acts points toward a universal gospel intended for all, including slaves.

The term *training* in verse 12 may be a reference to the

catechetical training that accompanies preparation for baptism. The training leads people to forego false religion, or no religion at all, for the high-minded Christian religion, as well as to eliminate baser actions.

The Christian lives soberly in relation to self, uprightly or sensibly in relation to others with respect for their rights, and with an authentic piety in relation to God.

All three of these relationships are in this world, that is, in the present time (1 Timothy 6:17; 2 Timothy 4:10).

In verse 13, however, the Christian perspective is greater than an inheritance from the past and a strong moral commitment in the present. Christians envision life within the context of eternity. Christians await a time when all that is good will be brought to its full and complete end (see 1 Corinthians 1:7).

The word *appearance* is also used when speaking of the arrival of a Roman official. The subtle suggestion may be that Jesus is the true ruler who will appear, and the true Kingdom will finally be established.

The verse contains a section that is difficult to translate. It sounds as if this could read *God* [who is] *Savior Jesus Christ*. At no other time does Paul ever refer to Christ as God, though in the Pastoral Letters God and Christ are placed side by side (1 Timothy 1:1; 5:21; 6:13; 2 Timothy 1:1; 4:1; Titus 3:4-6). The RSV note indicates a variant translation, *of the great God and our Savior*, eliminating the difficulty by making the two very distinct entities.

The description *great God* establishes a clear distinction between the Christian/biblical God and the claims made by heathen religion regarding its gods and goddesses. Paul had refuted this sort of claim during his missionary activity in Ephesus (Acts 19:26).

Having declared God's intention of salvation for all humankind and invested great hope in the teaching ministry of the church all within the context of eternity, now in verse 14 Paul alludes to the work of Christ.

Rescue is a dominant theme throughout the Bible. God

rescued the Hebrews from slavery, and redeemed them (Exodus 15:13). Following the defeat and subsequent deportation, God rescued the people from their captivity (Isaiah 44:23).

However, we should note that God rescues from the power of sin, not from the guilt that accompanies sin.

In the Hebrew mind, purification takes place after deliverance (Ezekiel 37:23). The same theme is picked up in 1 John 1:7.

The work of Christ, then, is to make a people for himself. The effort of God to make a chosen people stems from the earliest history of Israel (see Exodus 19:5, 6).

The Christian perspective is that the church has inherited the designation of God's people. The church is the new Israel (Galatians 6:16; Philippians 3:3). The same theme is reflected in 1 Peter 2:9, 10.

Wary of the pride that can develop along with the notion of being chosen, Paul hastens to add the description of God's chosen people. They are *zealous for good deeds*. Christianity at its best is not merely a systematized theological construction that interprets all of life, nor is it a people confident of their being a people in God's sight. True Christianity is also a way of life expressing itself through good works; it is a practical way of living.

Thus in verse 15 theological undergirding is given to the high calling of an exemplary moral life. All of these things, both moral expectation and theological understandings, must be taught. In 2:1 the same verb is used, *teach*.

The final sentence may be intended as much for Titus's congregation to hear as for Titus himself. Evidently some members of the congregation have been disregarding the teaching and admonition of the younger preacher. Here Paul tells them that they should not disregard the preacher's authority.

§ § § § § § §

The Message of Titus 2

The earliest Christian hope had little to do with transforming society or correcting social deficiencies. Instead, the Christian movement concentrated its energies on the identity of individuals as people of worth in the sight of God and people for whom Jesus of Nazareth gave his life. Somewhat disturbing to modern readers is the fact that the Pastoral Letters refuse to tackle the larger moral issues of social injustice to which much modern Christian energy is directed. What we often overlook, however, is the incredible power that the earliest Christians attributed to their exemplary behavior and attitude.

What else can we learn from this chapter?

§ The older members of the community need to be the wise ones with temperate judgment and insight.

§ Older members of any community have an educational responsibility to the younger members.

§ In all of our behavior we should be careful not to discredit the name of God.

§ We should examine currently popular morality or behavior to see if it corresponds to what has been found fundamentally sound over the course of years.

§ All members of the community have a high moral obligation.

§ Our behavior embodies and adorns our theological formulations.

§ God's intention is always to save.

§ Christians live life in the context of eternity and the hope of a returning Christ.

§ § § § § § §

Titus 3

Introduction to This Chapter

Recall that the letter to Titus begins with concerns about the internal organization of the Christian church on Crete. In Chapter 3 the transition has been made between internal organization and external ethical behavior required of Christians in society. In this chapter Titus learns of the relationships, ethical principles, and the motives which all Christians should understand in order to be the people of God in the midst of society. Paul addressed similar issues in Romans 13:1. All of Chapter 3 is similar to Romans 12:17–13:7, in that it emphasizes both respecting authority and the Christian duty to be useful citizens.

Here is an outline of Chapter 3.

 I. Responsibility to Civil Authorities (3:1-2)
 II. Reasons/Motives for Responsibilities (3:3-7)
III. Another "The Saying Is Sure" (3:8)
IV. What to Avoid (3:9-11)
 V. Final Personal Words and a Blessing (3:12-15)

Responsibility to Civil Authorities (3:1-2)

We have seen the concern for respect regarding government authority earlier in the Pastorals (1 Timothy 2:1-2). Paul is not the only writer with this concern. Similar caution is voiced in 1 Peter 3:8-17.

In all likelihood these cautions are responses to a real threat, not merely to a theoretical possibility. Evidently some Christians took their new commitment to Christ and the kingdom of God to the point of flouting the authority of Rome. In Acts we have intimations of the threat that the pagan culture felt from Christians. In Acts 17 Luke reports of Paul's ministry in Thessalonica. There he is accused as one of the men *who have turned the world upside down* (Acts 17:6). See also Acts 24:5.

Christians are to be ready for any good work. Note that Paul does not insist on exclusively Christian works. Paul is urging Christians to be willing to follow through on actions begun by government authorities. However, the term also implies the works that have been initiated by the Christian community.

The concern for public appearance in verse 2 occurs regularly in Paul's work. Recall that earlier he had counseled Timothy and the church not to be contentious or quarrelsome (see 1 Timothy 3:3; 2 Timothy 2:23-24). A similar concern occupies Paul's thought in Romans 12:18-21; however, here in Titus the tone seems more positive.

Gentleness is one of the keys to this section. Gentleness picks up on themes of Jesus, from the Sermon on the Mount (Matthew 5:5) and later (Matthew 11:29). Note that gentleness is not reserved for or restricted to those who have earned the respect of Christians, nor to those who are popular with Christians. Gentleness is to be characteristic of Christian relationships with all people. In a subtle way, Paul continues with the universal implications of the gospel. See also Galatians 6:10.

Recall that in 2:11 Paul had pointed to the human face of God through the manifestation of Christ. People cannot know a notion of grace without seeing what this grace looks like in real life. The surrounding pagan culture must see in the Christian community the grace of Christ. Throughout the Pastoral Epistles a major theme is the need to develop an essential integrity between theological/doctrinal statement and personal/corporate ethics and behavior. The Christian must be able to both talk the talk and walk the walk.

Reasons/Motives for Responsibilities (3:3-7)

Thus far Paul has given sound advice to a minority group that needs to protect itself against misunderstanding and potential persecution. In one sense the counsel is sheer pragmatic wisdom. What makes it distinctly Christian is the additional motive that Paul states in verse 3.

Christian motive takes its cue from two facts. First, we ourselves are no better than the people on whom we look. Deep in the tradition of Israel a similar insight is preserved (Exodus 22:21). This counsel also takes its cue from Jesus' encounter with the woman of the city who wept over his feet. Recall that the parable of the two debtors (Luke 7:40-50) poignantly illustrates that we have all been forgiven many times over and should, therefore, ourselves be forgiving. Furthermore, Paul may be reflecting on his own experience (1 Corinthians 15:9).

Second, Christians have been the fortunate recipients of God's graciousness and kindness. In the letter to the Ephesians Paul includes substantial reiteration of what appears in Titus (Ephesians 2:3-10; 4:17-24; and 5:1-2). There he describes the Christian's former life and God's gifts (4:22-24).

Foolish refers to errors in intellectual thought (see Romans 1:21; Ephesians 4:18).

Disobedient refers to deliberate action resulting from the will, primarily with respect to human authority, as in *disobedient to parents* (Romans 1:30). The word is used with regard to divine authority as well (see Titus 1:16).

Led astray describes the senselessness to which they had fallen prey. The description reveals the presence and very real threat of false teachers.

Slaves to various passions describes the disobedience.

The result of disobedience and being led astray by false

teachers is quite predictable. People have become involved in all imaginable antisocial behavior. Antisocial behavior is in part the subject of another letter as well (see 1 Peter 2:1).

In sharp contrast with what human beings are inclined to do, *goodness* and *loving kindness* in verse 4 characterize God's action toward the creation.

The term used to describe kindness is the same term used to describe the natives' treatment of Paul on the island of Malta (Acts 28:2). The term in the Greek language is *philanthropia*, from which we have the word *philanthropy*.

The goodness and lovingkindness of God *appeared* in Jesus (recall 2:11), through whom we know of God's compassion and goodness.

Note in verse 5 that the appearance of God through Christ follows immediately the description of human sinfulness and sin's impact on society. This placement is not merely accidental. Paul implies that the appearance has nothing to do with people earning God's gifts. Indeed, the epiphany/manifestation of God is solely on God's initiative. The propensity to assume one's goodness as the initiative for God's action runs deeply within the human spirit.

The virtue of God's compassion is God's virtue. The problem of Pharisaism is not solely a Jewish problem. The inclination toward religious and national pride is a thoroughly, and universal, human predicament. To the Ephesians Paul gives a corrective (see Ephesians 2:8-9). In 2 Timothy a similar corrective has already been noted (1:9).

The *washing of regeneration* refers to baptism. The word *regeneration* is used here, for the only time in the New Testament, to refer to spiritual rebirth.

Other possibilities for the meaning include Jewish usage by rabbis to describe a convert from paganism to Judaism. Some of the Greek mystery religions used the term to describe initiation into a sect. Stoics also used the term to describe the periodic cycles of life.

Paul speaks of baptism as the means by which we enter into the new life of Christ (Romans 6:4). The use of the term *baptism* evokes two images. One is the washing away of sins. In his third explanation of his conversion, Paul recalls the dramatic conversation with Ananias (Acts 22:16). The same image is repeated in Ephesians 5:26. The other image is of rebirth in the well-known encounter between Jesus and Nicodemus in John 3:5.

Renewal is also mentioned in Romans 12:2. This term does not suggest a polishing up of something that is already present. Paul's usage implies a radical new order of living (see 2 Corinthians 5:17).

A careful reading of this text suggests a corrective to any who would make baptism conditional upon the attitude or the achievement of the one being baptized. Indeed, this text suggests the radical transforming power of baptism.

Poured out in verse 6 recalls the Old Testament prophet Joel (Joel 2:28-29), and the day of Pentecost (Acts 2:17). Pentecost, when viewed from this perspective, is not a once-in-history event. Rather, the presence of the Spirit is an ongoing truth for the Christian following baptism.

Paul describes God's mercy as rich: *God, who is rich in mercy, out of the great love with which he loved us* (Ephesians 2:4).

The purpose of God's mercy follows in verse 7. The justification of the Christian is not reserved for life after the last breath has been breathed. Justification is the beginning of the Christian life.

Christians are heirs in hope of eternal life (Galatians 4:7). To the Romans Paul made a similar claim: *It is the Spirit himself bearing witness with our spirit that we are children of God, and if children, then heirs, heirs of God and fellow heirs with Christ* (8:16, 17).

The Christian hope is eternal life.

Another "The Saying Is Sure" (3:8)

Faithful is the word repeats the formula sayings peculiar to the Pastoral Epistles (recall 1 Timothy 1:15; 3:1; 4:9; 2 Timothy 2:11). Since Paul is talking about baptism, the phrase may be excerpted from a baptismal rite.

To what does the saying refer? Is attention being drawn to what has preceded or to what will follow? In earlier usages the term meant that the entire gospel that has been entrusted to the apostle is trustworthy. The phrase may also allude to the characteristics summarized in verses 4-7 or possibly the commands that had been given in 2:1–3:3.

What to Avoid (3:9-11)

Without further explanation, the letter continues with renewed emphasis on Christian ethics. The RSV notes that another translation is possible, suggesting that the Christian's responsibilities include pursuit of honorable occupations. To the Thessalonians, some of whom had become a public scandal due to their refusal to work in anticipation of an imminent return of Christ, Paul charged that they should *aspire to live quietly, to mind your own affairs, and to work with your hands* (1 Thessalonians 4:11). The instruction may also include the general thought that Christians should pursue anything that is good (recall 2:14; 3:2).

The implication is also made that the truths of the Christian gospel are themselves good and useful (1 Timothy 4:8; 2 Timothy 3:16).

When the Christian individual channels energies into creative and good efforts, certain behaviors detrimental to both the gospel and society will be avoided. The church is to avoid stupid controversies. Another translation for this term is *foolish speculations* (recall 1 Timothy 1:4; 6:4; 2 Timothy 2:23).

Endless preoccupation with genealogies has been mentioned in 1 Timothy 1:4.

Dissension plagues the Christian movement, as does the stubborn heritage of discussion about the law. With a single stroke Paul discards them as being entirely unprofitable and futile.

The word *factious* in verse 10 appears only here in the New Testament. The term may refer to separatists or rigid sectarians. Paul has little use for individuals or small groups of people in the church who would dare restrict the truth of God to their truth. Throughout the Book of Acts the Christian movement struggles against such sectarians. At the crucial Jerusalem conference *some believers who belonged to the party of the Pharisees rose up, and said, "It is necessary to circumcise . . . and to charge . . . to keep the law of Moses"* (Acts 15:5). Paul recognizes the inevitability of small groups in the church (see 1 Corinthians 11:19).

Paul recalls admonishing people in private. *For three years I did not cease night or day to admonish everyone with tears* (Acts 20:31). However, Paul was willing to admonish through public confrontation as well (see 2 Thessalonians 3:14-15).

The technique may also be based on Jesus' instructions in Matthew 18:15-17. *If your brother sins against you, go and tell him his fault, between you and him alone. . . . If he does not listen, take one or two others along with you, that every word may be confirmed by the evidence of two or three witnesses. If he refuses to listen to them, tell it to the church; and if he refuses to listen even to the church, let him be to you as a Gentile and a tax collector.* See also 2 John 10. The early church is determined to avoid any who would imperil the Christian movement.

Perverted in verse 11 means twisted, beyond recovery. The sins of the sectarians include not only their sectarianism but also their refusal to heed wise counsel. The statement sounds like a resignation to the fact that with some individuals nothing can be done. They are bound to create dissension within the congregation.

Doubtless some of the other members will want to press the attack and condemn the wrongdoers themselves. Paul understands the latent impulse. He counters by holding to the sectarians already being condemned by their own actions. These people can be left, and are better left, to God's judgment.

The individual is also condemned by his own conscience. The same word is used in the parable of the talents. *I will condemn you out of your own mouth, you wicked servant!* (Luke 19:22).

Final Personal Words and a Blessing (3:12-15)

The letter concludes with personal greetings and requests and a benediction.

In verse 12 *Artemas* may be an abbreviated form of Artemidorus. According to a later tradition, he was one of the seventy (Luke 10:1) and later became one of the bishops of Lystra.

Tychicus of Asia is mentioned in 2 Timothy 4:12 and Acts 20:4. Later he appears as a messenger of Paul's. *Tychicus will tell you all about my affairs* (Colossians 4:7).

Nicopolis is a name of many cities. The name means *victory town*. The town to which Paul calls attention is probably in Epirus, a center for missionary work in the region of Dalmatia. The city had been established by Octavian in 31 B.C. The location of the city makes it readily accessible from the Adriatic on a journey to Rome.

Zenas in verse 13 is a Greek name, though he is identified as a lawyer, thus indicating that he may have been a convert to Christianity from Judaism. Later tradition holds that he was the author of the apocryphal *Acts of Titus.*

Apollos is mentioned along with Zenas. The name is a very common one. He is mentioned in Acts 18:24 and also in 1 Corinthians 1:12; 16:12.

Recall that among the qualifications for a bishop is extending hospitality to travelers. Here, Titus is requested to see to it that the men are not lacking in anything.

In case the congregation has not already understood that the instructions are not restricted solely to Titus, the letter now, in verse 14, expands its appeal to all Christians in the household.

In his letter to the Romans Paul indicates his concern that Christians show some practical manifestation of the work of God through Christ (see Romans 7:4). Elsewhere in the New Testament: *For if these things are yours and abound, they keep you from being ineffective or unfruitful in the knowledge of our Lord Jesus Christ* (2 Peter 1:8).

The concluding caution regarding unfruitfulness may also be in response to charges made by antagonists of the Christian movement who believed that Christians were dangerous and a threat to society.

Unnamed other companions also send greetings in verse 15.

Greetings are to be extended only to other Christians, not to false teachers or sectarians intent on dividing the church. Real friends are those who share the Christian faith and have common loyalty to Christ. The instruction to greet many implies Paul's tacit approval and understanding that the letter will be read not only by Titus as a private letter but also to the gathering, probably in public worship.

Grace also extends to the entire community.

§ § § § § § §

The Message of Titus 3

The letter to Titus begins with instructions to a single
preacher and ends with greetings to the entire church.
The transition from an individual preacher to the
formation and regular gathering of a Christian community
is precisely what Titus must make. The transition that
will be accomplished is the movement from doctrine
through to new ethical orientations and a new manner of
life. We will be closer to the dynamic life of this letter if
we can see not only Titus but also the congregation
purposely working to link their thinking with their doing,
their theology with their actions in society.

What else can we learn from this chapter?

§ The Christian faith is one not only of high spiritual
character, but one of humble obedience as well.

§ Christians can be compassionate because they can
recall a time when they were as bad as the worst they see
in society.

§ God's gracious work on our behalf is due to God's
grace and initiative, not our merit.

§ A radically Christian stance is that even our
repentance is not sufficient to merit God's grace.

§ Through Christ we become sons and daughters of
God and can share in, as well as anticipate, eternal life.

§ Christians must be certain that whatever they expect
of others, they themselves do.

§ Not only does God work with a few who are famous;
God works with the anonymous as well.

§ The church is the place where high character is
developed.

§ § § § § § §

Philemon

Introduction to This Chapter

The letter to Philemon is, like the Pastoral Epistles, a personal letter written by Paul. The immediate reason for the letter is that an escaped slave, Onesimus, is now a trusted helper for the imprisoned apostle. Paul writes to the slave's owner, Philemon, with a remarkable request. Paul wants Philemon not only to refrain from punishing the escaped slave but also to receive him back graciously. At least one interpreter suggests that Paul implies even more than this. According to this interpretation, Paul desires Philemon to release Onesimus from slavery altogether so that Onesimus can stay with Paul as his trusted assistant during the very trying period of Paul's own imprisonment. Most interpreters do not subscribe to such a radical interpretation.

Paul writes the letter while in prison (verse 1), probably the period of house arrest in Rome sometime during the years A.D 61–63. His other letters are addressed to churches (Romans 1:7; 1 Corinthians 1:2; 2 Corinthians 1:1; Galatians 1:2; Ephesians 1:1; Philippians 1:1; Colossians 1:2; 1 Thessalonians 1:1; 2 Thessalonians 1:1). We have already seen how the Pastoral Epistles, which were written ostensibly to individuals, were also intended for a wider reading.

As has already been pointed out in the Introduction to the Pastoral Epistles, Paul adopts/appropriates from the predominant culture the form of correspondence in common usage at that time. The standard form included:

(1) opening: including the sender's name, the recipient's name, a greeting;

(2) thanksgiving or blessing, very often with prayers of intercession;

(3) body: the actual content/reason for the writing, frequently including future plans;

(4) parenesis (instructions/requests);

(5) closing: usually standard forms of benedictions and greetings. Occasionally mention is made of the actual writing process itself (see, for example, 2 Thessalonians 3:17).

The structure of Philemon is as follows:

(1) opening (verses 1-3): sender, *Paul*; recipient, *Philemon, our beloved worker*; greeting, *grace to you and peace from God our Father and the Lord Jesus Christ.*

(2) thanksgiving (verses 4-7): *I thank my God always when I remember you in my prayers . . . I pray that the sharing of your faith may promote the knowledge of all the good that is ours in Christ.*

(3) body (verses 8-20): *I appeal to you for my child, Onesimus.*

(4) parenesis—final instructions (verses 7-22): *receive him . . . charge to my account . . . Refresh my heart in Christ . . . prepare a room for me.*

(5) closing (verses 23-25): greetings, closing benediction.

One of the ironies of history is that Paul was hardly a systematic theologian whose primary aim was to state in well-rounded thinking a systematic examination of the gospel of Christ. All of Paul's letters are written to specific congregations or specific individuals who are wrestling with difficulties or stresses that have come up during the course of normal personal and corporate life together. Paul writes as a pastor attempting to bring every facet of life into the perspective of the work of God through Christ.

Modern readers will at once be struck by Paul's

seeming lack of concern for the reprehensible but socially acceptable standard of slavery. Why doesn't the apostle address the issue?

The first reason Paul does not attack the institution of slavery is that slavery had long since become a major part of the Roman Empire's culture. In fact, slavery had become a predominant means of labor. Roman practice included slaves in nearly every aspect of labor, from the most menial tasks to the higher responsibilities. Wealthy people would often have a large number of slaves that would care for every detail of family life. Slaves were frequently artists, painters, architects, librarians, even doctors. Slavery was intertwined with every aspect of culture. In short, slavery was a fact of life as readily accepted as Roman rule itself.

This is not to suggest that slavery in the Roman practice was a positive institution. A slave had no rights. Indeed, a slave was little more than another object in the owner's inventory of possessions to be considered along with wagons, cattle, and household goods. The slave's entire life lay within the authority of the owner. Marriage was not a right. Punishments were entirely up to the owner; there was no recourse for the slave. Punishments varied. Frequently slaves were branded on the forehead, or forced to carry a *fucra*—a V-shaped instrument of torture. Occasionally slaves were the playthings of cruel owners and were forced to fight animals in an arena. One incident gives stark evidence of how precarious the slave's life could be. A record exists of how one slave was crucified for no more reason than for the master's own pleasure. No more reason was required! Had the Christian movement arbitrarily attacked the detestable institution, the church could easily have become the target of immeasurable censure and attack by a threatened society and government.

A more subtle reason can be discerned as well. The moral implications of slavery include poor self-esteem, identity as something other than fully human, and a coarseness of soul that renders any vulnerability or compassion impossible. The Christian movement hardly stood by with nothing to say. Indeed, the movement was a radically transforming movement, but not in public and immediately social manifestations. Rather, the movement emphasized the change that occurred within the human soul with respect to identity, self-esteem, and community. Jesus' teachings include respect for every human life. *Look at the birds of the air: they neither sow nor reap nor gather into barns, and yet your heavenly Father feeds them. Are you not of more value than they?* (Matthew 6:26). Many of Jesus' parables dealt with the importance of one. Recall the parables of the lost sheep and the woman who had lost one coin (Luke 15:3-10).

Paul himself refuses to see slaves as anything but people. They are certainly not mere property (Philemon 10). Granted, slaves still have certain responsibilities to their masters, but by the same token Christian masters also have responsibilities toward their slaves (Ephesians 6:9; Colossians 4:1).

In Paul's thinking, the distinction between slave and free man or woman—so strongly marked in society—has begun to fade (1 Corinthians 12:13). To the Galatians Paul asserts, *There is neither Jew nor Greek, there is neither slave nor free, there is neither male nor female; for you are all one in Christ Jesus* (3:28).

It appears almost incredible to the modern reader, but Paul sees the social and cultural institution as a given, and as such an appropriate place in which the Christian gospel should be lived out (1 Corinthians 7:21-24). To the slaves in Ephesus he charges, *Slaves, be obedient to those who are your earthly masters . . . as to Christ . . . rendering service with a good will as to the Lord and not to men* (6:5-6).

Paul's extraordinary request depends not only upon Philemon's own Christian convictions but also upon the relationship that the two men have. Paul himself characterizes the relationship in warm terms: *beloved fellow worker* (verse 1), *your partner* (verse 17), and in his final instructions requests a guest room to be readied (verse 22). This closeness comes as no surprise, since Philemon had been converted to Christianity through Paul's ministry in Ephesus. Remember that while in Ephesus Paul had to leave the synagogue. People from the surrounding country went there to hear him (Acts 19:9-10). From the evidence in the letter, we see that Philemon had assumed a major leadership role in the church. The church met in Philemon's home: *the church in your house* (verse 2).

Here is an outline of Philemon.

I. Introductory Opening (verses 1-3)
II. Thanksgiving (verses 4-7)
III. Paul's Remarkable Request (verses 8-20)
IV. Final Instructions (verses 21-22)
V. Closing Salutations (verses 23-25)

Introductory Opening (verses 1-3)

As a matter of first priority in all of his other letters, Paul establishes his authority at the outset. We have already seen in the Pastoral Epistles Paul's declaration of his being an apostle (1 Timothy 1:1; 2 Timothy 1:1; Titus 1:1). In the balance of his correspondence he does the same, with the only exception being First and Second Thessalonians (see Romans 1:1; 1 Corinthians 1:1; 2 Corinthians 1:1; Galatians 1:1; Ephesians 1:1; Philippians 1:1; Colossians 1:1).

To Philemon, however, he makes no such reference or claim. Paul identifies himself only as a prisoner *for* Christ Jesus. In Ephesians 3:1 he also refers to himself as a prisoner for Christ Jesus. The first few words of the letter establish both tone and intention. The tone of the letter, then, is very personal, with no trappings of authority. The tone is one of shared enslavement and victory. As Onesimus is enslaved, so is Paul. Paul goes on to contend, though in a very subtle way, that he is not enslaved primarily by his chains and imprisonment. Instead, his imprisonment is for Christ. Paul refuses to allow his outward circumstances to dictate who he is and what he is doing. His witness to the Corinthians is *thanks be to God, who in Christ always leads us in triumph* (2 Corinthians 2:14). God's intention of spreading the gospel will not be stopped by the arbitrary decision of Rome to imprison Paul.

Philemon is identified as *our beloved fellow worker*. *Beloved* is used to describe both Barnabas and Paul during the Jerusalem conference (Acts 15:25). The word has powerful connotations. Is Paul suggesting that if Philemon is a beloved fellow worker, then he is bound to release the escaped slave? Perhaps Paul means that Philemon should release Onesimus for work as a preacher in service to the gospel.

Timothy is frequently associated with Paul. His name is mentioned in Second Corinthians, Philippians, Colossians, First and Second Thessalonians, and the Pastoral Epistles. Timothy is not called an apostle. In the Book of Acts one of the absolute qualifications for apostleship is that the individual must have been an eyewitness to the resurrected Christ. Timothy was a later convert and thus did not fulfill the requirement.

But since the letter is a very personal letter, why is Timothy's name mentioned? Two possibilities emerge. First, Philemon may have a special relationship with Timothy about which we know little. The second suggestion comes from the subsequent people identified. Note that Timothy is called *our brother*, Apphia is *our sister*, Archippus is *our fellow soldier*. Paul uses plural pronouns in a personal letter. Could it be that Paul is exerting a very strong yet subtle pressure on Philemon? Is Paul working with the assumption that even the most personal letter will eventually be read in the context of the entire church gathered in Philemon's house?

Here we have a rich suggestion as to the power and importance of the church. Philemon will feel two immense forces acting upon him as he wrestles with his decision regarding the escaped slave. First, he will feel the pressure of the entire congregation on him to make the "right" decision, to do as Paul requests. If he does not make that decision, not only will Paul, Onesimus, and Philemon know, but also the entire congregation will know. We may want to characterize this pressure as peer pressure within the church for individuals to conform to the highest Christian aspirations.

Equally important, however, is the fact that Philemon, if he chooses to do as Paul requests, will be going against the grain of social and cultural expectation. He will be making a decision as a minority. In that circumstance, he will need all the moral support he can find. The church will provide that necessary support for him.

Therefore, in verse 2 Paul mentions other individuals, all of whom have some significance for Philemon.

Apphia is a Phrygian name. Since her name appears along with Archippus, some interpreters hold that she is the wife of Philemon and that Onesimus is, therefore, an escaped household slave about whom they are both concerned. *Sister* in this verse should be understood in the Christian context of a sister in Christ.

Archippus, according to one interpretation, is the son of Philemon and Apphia. However, since his name appears in Colossians 4:17 with the instructions *See that you fulfill the ministry which you have received in the Lord*, he may well have been an officer in the house church that met in Philemon's home. If this is the case, then he will be a part of the congregation that will oversee the decision Philemon makes regarding the returning slave.

To the church in your house reveals the early center of the Christian movement. In the first generations of Christianity, there were no church buildings. Even if there had been buildings, large gatherings of Christians would have appeared to be a threat to Roman authority. Therefore, churches were relatively small gatherings of Christians in people's homes (Romans 16:5; 1 Corinthians 16:19).

The original word for church, *ecclesia*, combines two ideas of a people called out as well as the people gathered for religious purposes. In the Book of Acts the term is used to describe the unique Christian movement that had developed from within Israel (Acts 8:1; 12:1). James uses the word *assembly* for the church (James 2:2).

Though the letter is addressed to a single individual, Paul's careful use of plural words implies that whatever he says and whatever Philemon decides will have an impact on the entire Christian ecclesia/church.

Paul concludes the introductory greeting in verse 3 with two special words: *grace* and *peace*. Grace at its root means that which can bring joy or pleasure. The Christian meaning of the term comes from the absolutely free gift-giving of God.

Peace in the Christian context means a condition that can only occur when hostility between God and human beings has ceased. At its root, peace has to do with the reconciliation that has been accomplished by the will of God and the work of Christ.

Thanksgiving (verses 4-7)

The thanksgiving in this letter is longer than the thanksgiving in other letters; compare it for instance with Philippians 1:3-11; Colossians 1:3-8; and 1 Thessalonians 1:2-5.

The word for *thanksgiving* is the same word from which we have the word *eucharist*.

Paul uses the very personal expression *my God* as he does in Philippians 1:3, *I thank my God in all my remembrance of you.*

As in other letters, Paul uses the word *always* with thanks (see Romans 1:8-10; 1 Corinthians 1:4; Colossians

1:3). Thanks are always given to God for what God has been able to effect in Philemon's life. Paul has heard of the work God has effected, perhaps through Epaphras (see Colossians 1:7-8; 4:12). Paul may also have heard of Philemon's witness through the escaped slave.

Philemon's love and faith are expressed in two directions in verse 5. The first is toward the Lord Jesus Christ. However, Christian love is always expressed toward others as well. The Christian faith is *faith working* (*made effective*, according to the RSV note) *through love* (Galatians 5:6). Philemon's love has been expressed toward the congregation that meets in his home.

Paul stresses the relationship Philemon has with Christ. The implication of Paul's carefully chosen words is that a relationship with Christ is of primary importance. Authentic love toward others depends upon relationship with Christ.

In verse 6 Paul gives the reason for his prayer of intercession. Unfortunately, the English translation does not include a very special word. In the Greek language, the verse centers on the *koinonia*, the active communal participation of Christians in faith and love. Paul's prayer is for the Christian fellowship, the *koinonia*, that it will increase (*promote*) knowledge of God.

The knowledge for which Paul prays is more than intellectual grasp. Knowledge in the Christian context includes understanding of the gospel, of the ethical principles involved in Christian witness, of the principles of fellowship (*koinonia*). In short, understanding means having the mind of Christ in all things. Paul regularly prays for each church to gain in Christian knowledge. Paul prays for the Philippian church (Philippians 1:9). For other examples see Colossians 1:9-10; and Ephesians 1:16-17. In a similar vein Paul prays for the church in Rome: *Be transformed by the renewal of your mind* (Romans 12:2).

Knowledge is always in conjunction with the good that

God intends and that Christians can do. Recall the recurrent emphasis in the Pastoral Epistles on a Christian faith that evidences itself in works of charity.

The verse concludes with the focus on Christ. All knowledge and good are for the glory of Christ. Paul is setting the stage for his incredible request. By implication, the decision that Philemon will have to make will also be for the glory of Christ.

We have seen through various references to other letters that what Paul has said to this point in large measure has been said to other Christians as well as Philemon. Now Paul points to specific reasons for his thanksgiving (initiated in verse 4) for Philemon, whom he calls *brother*.

We may wish that Paul had been specific not only in name but also in listing Philemon's various ministries. We have only Paul's conclusion, that many of the brethren have had their hearts refreshed through Philemon's work. The word used to describe Philemon's refreshment is the same word used by Jesus in offering rest to the weary (Matthew 11:28-29).

The word *heart* will form a link between Onesimus, Paul, and Philemon. In verse 12 Paul will claim that Onesimus is Paul's *very heart*. In verse 20 Paul will ask Philemon to refresh his heart as Philemon had refreshed the hearts of innumerable members of the church.

Paul's Remarkable Request (verses 8-20)

All that has preceded has set the stage for Paul's incredible request. Paul's request is essentially an intercession on behalf of an escaped slave who, according to Roman law, has absolutely no recourse once he confronts his master.

The request itself consists of three sections. First, Paul summarizes his own dilemma. Should he summon up all of his apostolic authority? Or should he instead rely upon the best judgment and Christian convictions of another man (verses 8-12)? Second, he gives a brief summary of how he came into contact with Onesimus (verses 13-16). Finally, he makes his request (verses 17-20).

Anyone who has read Paul's correspondence knows that he is hardly timid when it comes to his work. However, his confidence is not something that comes from a strong ego or overt power. Instead, his confidence stems from his relationship to God through Christ.

Moreover, Paul's boldness with Philemon has its foundation in Philemon's conversion to Christ through Paul's ministry (verse 19).

Paul presumes that he could use all the force of his apostolic authority in making the request. In that case, the request would have had the power of an official order. At one point Paul reminds the Corinthians that he is not issuing commands (2 Corinthians 8:8).

The phrase *what is required* implies a standard or norm of ethical behavior that is the duty of the Christian. Obviously what is required according to Roman law and cultural custom would have been a punishment and/or execution. Therefore, Paul lifts Philemon's sights to the highest Christian ethic. The same term is used in Paul's charge to wives in Colossians 3:18, and his imperative to the Ephesians that *there be no filthiness, nor silly talk, nor levity, which are not fitting* (5:4).

Paul recognizes in verse 9 that a gift, in order to be authentic, is never attained through force of any kind.

The special love of which Paul speaks is the love that characterizes God's care for humanity and, therefore, is characteristic among Christians: *agape.*

The Greek word translated *ambassador* is also the word for *an old man* (see the RSV note). The alternate translation is more consistent with the tone of the letter. Paul writes as an older, wiser man who is now a prisoner for Christ. The wording implies Paul's imprisonment due to the will of Christ and not to action of government officials.

Our familiarity with the letter prevents us from seeing the immense drama being played out in written words. Nowhere is the drama any greater than in verse 10. In the Greek language the slave's name does not appear immediately. *I beseech thee concerning my child, whom I begat in my bonds, Onesimus.* Notice the sense of hesitancy. Paul initiates his request with descriptions. *My child* is reminiscent of the letters to Timothy (recall 1 Timothy 1:2, 18; 2 Timothy 2:1). To the Corinthians and Galatians Paul uses the same term to describe his relationship to the congregation (1 Corinthians 4:14; Galatians 4:19).

Evidently Onesimus met Paul while Paul was in prison. As a result of their relationship, the slave was converted to Christianity. Paul states that he is the instrument through which Onesimus was converted. A parallel usage occurs in 1 Corinthians 4:15.

The name *Onesimus* is a very common slave name, as it implies usefulness. Though not apparent in the English, in Greek the name Onesimus affords Paul a play on words in verse 11. Parenthetically, Paul comments on how the one named useful was quite useless. Now the one named useful will indeed be useful. What has made the difference? Onesimus has become a Christian and thus he is now useful both in name and in fact. Furthermore, Onesimus is helpful not only to his legal owner, Philemon, but also to Paul.

How is Onesimus helpful to both men? Paul may be alluding to the kind ministries of personal service that the slave has given to Paul in his imprisonment. Since he is now a Christian, Onesimus will be of much higher character and service (see Ephesians 6:5). In addition, Paul may be alluding to the fact that in Onesimus he has an excellent example of how successful the Christian missionary movement can be.

Legally Paul must return the escaped slave. However, in verse 12, he returns him not merely as another slave in the empire who has attempted to flee from a master. Paul sends the man very much as an extension of himself. In the original Greek the word is *bowels*. The RSV translates this into *heart*. The point is that Paul has very deep personal feelings and commitments to Onesimus. When Onesimus arrives in Philemon's house, it will be as if Paul himself has arrived.

The decision to send Onesimus back has been a very difficult one. Indeed, Paul has given much thought to retaining the slave for himself. Paul's consideration in verse 13 is tactfully set in the context of what Philemon would have done had he been with Paul. Surely Philemon would have wanted to help Paul. But in Philemon's absence his slave Onesimus has performed a similar service. The thought concludes with Paul's reiteration of verses 9 and 10, that is, a prisoner, a status that coincides with Onesimus' status. The two men are not significantly different. Both are servants of Christ.

In verse 14, however strong Paul's argument may have been, and even though Paul may have been able to resort to apostolic authority if need be, he refuses to act without the consent of Philemon. The ultimate decision must be made by Philemon himself.

Paul continues in verse 15 with a suggestion as to why the slave left Philemon in the first place. Recall that Paul has declared to the Romans *in everything God works for good with those who love him, who are called according to his purpose* (8:28). Could divine providence be at work even in this awkward and very volatile circumstance? Most readers quickly assume that the slave ran away. But at no time does Paul describe the slave's absence as a running away. Paul's suggestion is much more ambiguous.

The entire relationship between the master and the slave has changed in verse 16. Both men are now brothers in Christ (see the image in (Colossians 3:11).

Note that Paul does not try to argue the point. He makes no reference to what Philemon's own perspective might be. Instead, Paul assumes this perspective to be a matter of fact.

The relationship between Onesimus and Philemon will be on a much higher plane. Previously their relationship had been based on sheer economics and power of position. Now their relationship is through Christ.

The request concludes in verse 17 with Paul's reminder to Philemon that they are indeed partners in ministry as he had implied in verses 11 and 12. Of course, the relationship between Paul and Philemon is a Christian relationship.

Receive him suggests two possibilities. The first is that Philemon will receive the returning slave as a Christian brother without punishment or chastisement. Paul may also be asking Philemon to bring Onesimus into the membership of the church in his house.

As if signing an IOU, Paul states in verse 19 that this letter is in his own hand. Paul is not under coercion to say this. Thus Paul implies his own willingness to express concern for the slave above and beyond what would be normal behavior. But how will Paul repay? He is in prison with little prospect for immediate release. Perhaps Paul knows that Philemon will never make the claim. Perhaps Paul has some money remaining from the various love offerings that have been given to him by caring Christians.

Furthermore, Paul picks up on the theme of indebtedness by alluding to Philemon's indebtedness to Paul. Evidently Paul hesitates in saying this. Is he adding too much to the already moving and powerful request? But he does state the fact that Philemon himself owes his own Christian conversion to the ministry of Paul.

In the warmest term, *brother*, Paul indicates in verse 20 that he wants to see confirmation of the request first stated in verse 7. The emphasis is not on Paul. Instead, the emphasis is clearly on Onesimus, since the word for *benefit* in the Greek language is a word that sounds like Onesimus.

Final Instructions (verses 21-22)

Paul had begun by deliberately avoiding using his authority as an apostle. He would not command Philemon to do anything. Therefore, when he concludes by affirming his conviction that Philemon will indeed obey the request, Paul is referring to obedience to what the gospel itself demands of the disciple. The authority for Paul's request is nothing less than the Christian gospel. Paul recognizes the inclination to obey the higher authority in Philemon and thus concludes with the gracious note that Philemon will probably do even more than Paul has requested.

In verse 22 Paul hopes for release in the near future. In the Philippian letter he indicates this hope (Philippians 2:24). Recall that among the requirements for Christian leaders listed in the correspondence with Timothy is hospitality. Here Paul requests arrangements for a visit.

Closing Salutations (verses 23-25)

All the individuals mentioned are listed in Colossians. Epaphras is Paul's delegate to the church at Colossae whom Paul characterizes as *our beloved fellow servant . . . a faithful minister of Christ on our behalf* (Colossians 1:7).

Mark is probably John Mark (Acts 12:12, 25; 15:37). His name has not been mentioned since the separation in Acts 15:39. In Colossians 4:10 he is identified as Barnabas's cousin. He is commended to the churches in Colossae.

Aristarchus, born a Thessalonian (Acts 27:2), is one of Paul's conservative colleagues identified as such in Colossians 4:10-11. He accompanied Paul on his return journey through Macedonia to Troas (Acts 20:4).

Demas is mentioned in two other locations, first along with Luke in Colossians 4:14 and later as one who fell in love with the world and deserted Paul in 2 Timothy 4:10. Here Paul refers to Demas as a fellow worker.

Luke first appears with Paul in Acts 16:10. Evidently he

remained in Philippi after Paul's departure but was there when Paul visited some years later (Acts 20:5-6). He accompanies Paul to Jerusalem (Acts 21:15) and later appears again at Caesarea (Acts 27:2). Presumably Luke accompanies Paul on the final journey to Rome.

§ § § § § § §

The Message of Philemon

In this extraordinary personal letter, Paul makes an enormous request. He asks Philemon to forego every societal and legal precedent on behalf of an escaped slave. Paul dares appeal to the highest motive and the deepest commitments in a man who himself has been converted to Christ through Paul's ministry. Paramount in this letter is Paul's trust in the power of agape love, God's love, to dictate to an individual's conscience. What else can we learn from this letter?

§ We are not Christian in isolation; we are Christian in community with others.

§ The Christian thanks God through constant prayer for other Christians.

§ The good that is done by others gives us great joy and comfort.

§ Love cannot be coerced; love can only be evoked by the highest motive.

§ Christ gives us our highest motive to love unequivocally.

§ Our separations may be in some sense guided by providence to serve a higher or greater purpose.

§ Christian motive considers more than merely minimal action.

§ The church depends upon the grace of Christ for its life.

§ § § § § § §

Glossary of Terms

Agape: One of the many Greek words for love. Agape is the sort of love that God has for all people.

Alexander: Mentioned in 1 Timothy 1:19-20. Linked with Hymenaeus as one who had made a shipwreck of his faith. He is often identified with Alexander the coppersmith who had been a witness against Paul.

Apocalyptic: A type of religious thought that became particularly prevalent during times of extreme duress and persecution. Apocalyptic imagery includes cosmic confrontation between God and the power of evil.

Apollos: An influential Christian mentioned in Titus. He also appears in Acts and especially in First Corinthians (1:12; 3:4-6, 22; 4:6; 16:12).

Apostle: In order to be an apostle, one had to have been an eyewitness to the resurrected Christ. The title occurs some seventy-nine times in the New Testament. Paul frequently identifies himself as an apostle with the commission to preach (1 Timothy 2:7).

Apphia: A Christian woman addressed in Philemon. Because her name appears with Philemon, she is sometimes thought to be Philemon's wife.

Archippus: Paul calls him a fellow soldier in Philemon 2. Sometimes interpreted to be Philemon's son.

Aristarchus: Is mentioned in Philemon 24 but also appears in Acts and Colossians. A Macedonian from Thessalonica who was arrested with Paul in Ephesus

(Acts 19:29; 20:4). Tradition holds that he died a martyr's death under Nero in Rome.

Artemas: Mentioned in Titus 3:12. An early Christian whom Paul intended to go to Crete to relieve Titus, freeing Titus to join Paul in Nicopolis.

Bishop: From the Greek word *episkopos* (1 Timothy 3:2; Titus 1:7), meaning overseer. The office of bishop was the highest in the Christian church.

Claudia: A Christian woman mentioned in 2 Timothy 4:21. She sent greetings to Timothy. Tradition holds that she was the mother of Linus and may have become the wife of Pudens.

Corinth: Mentioned in 2 Timothy 4:20, the city is the chief commercial city on the Isthmus of Corinth. It is the capital of the Roman province of Achaia and famous for its temple of Aphrodite and its one thousand temple prostitutes.

Crete: A large island in the eastern Mediterranean Sea. Titus was appointed to supervise the organization of its Christian churches and to defend Christianity against heretics (Titus 1:5-14).

Dalmatia: The southern portion of Illyricum mentioned in 2 Timothy 4:10. The region showed stubborn resistance to Roman rule.

Deacon: First mentioned in Acts 6:1-6 as servers. The term stems from the word *diakonia:* work. Deacons served as assistants to bishops/elders (1 Timothy 3:8-13).

Demas: He was a co-worker with Paul. In Philemon 24 he is identified as a fellow worker.

Elder: From the Greek word *presbutos;* the word can be translated as either an old man or an official of the church. As an official, the position is an ordained clergy with administrative and pastoral duties. The duties of elder and bishop overlap.

Epaphras: Mentioned in Philemon 23, he was a native of Colossae responsible for first spreading the gospel to the area of Laodicea and Hierapolis (Colossians 4:12-13). He is identified as a fellow prisoner with Paul.

Ephesus: A large seaport city of immense commercial and religious importance where Paul spent a period of three years (Acts 19:8-10; 20:31).

Erastus: In 2 Timothy 4:20 and Acts 19:22 he is listed as a companion with Paul. Some interpreters hold that he was the treasurer of the city of Corinth.

Eubulus: In 2 Timothy 4:21 he is one of the Christians who send greetings to Timothy.

Galatia: Mentioned in 2 Timothy 4:10. Both a region and a Roman province in central Asia Minor.

Hymenaeus: In 1 Timothy 1:19 he is characterized as made a shipwreck of his faith. Paul recommends that he be excommunicated from the church. In 2 Timothy 2:17-18 he is associated with the Gnostic heretics who hold that the resurrection takes place at the time of Christian baptism.

Jannes and Jambres: According to Jewish legend the two magicians who challenged Moses and Aaron (Exodus 7:11-12, 22). They are characterized as the opponents to God's truth in 2 Timothy 3:8.

Linus: Mentioned in 2 Timothy 4:21. He is one of the Christian men who sends greetings to Timothy. According to tradition he became bishop in Rome.

Luke: Mentioned three times in the New Testament, two of which are in the Pastoral Epistles and Philemon (2 Timothy 4:11; Philemon 24). He is one of Paul's companions, and author of the third Gospel.

Marcion: In large measure this reformer of the second century contributed to the formation of the Christian canon. He accepted the Gospel of Luke and Paul's writings, while rejecting the Old Testament.

Mark: John Mark of Acts 13:13 who accompanies Paul on missionary work. He abandons Paul and Barnabas at Perga. In Philemon 24 he appears again, with the implication that there has been a reconciliation.

Nicopolis: The name means "City of Victory." Founded

by Octavian in 31 B.C., it is the city in which Paul intends to spend the winter (Titus 3:12).

Onesimus: A common slave name meaning *useful*. He is the escaped slave about whom Paul writes to Philemon. Tradition holds that he became bishop in Ephesus.

Parousia: The word that means both *presence* and *coming*. Christians used the term to describe the future, though imminent, coming of Christ.

Philemon: The eighteenth book of the New Testament. He is the Christian man to whom Paul writes with the extraordinary request that the escaped slave Onesimus be received as a fellow Christian.

Pudens: Mentioned in 2 Timothy 4:21; a Roman Christian who sends his greetings to Timothy.

Thessalonica: Mentioned in 2 Timothy 4:10, this city is where Paul established a church after he had been beaten in Philippi (Acts 16:22-24).

Timothy: The trusted friend and younger colleague of the Apostle Paul. He first appears in Acts 16 as the son of a Christian woman and heathen father. He is referred to as a brother in 1 Thessalonians 3:2. His task was to counteract heretics in Ephesus.

Titus: Another colleague of Paul whom Paul calls his true child in common faith (Titus 1:4). His assignment was to organize and supervise Cretan churches.

Trophimus: Mentioned in 2 Timothy 4:20; an Ephesian whom Paul met at Troas during the journey to Jerusalem (Acts 20:4-5). According to the letter to Timothy, he had been left ill at Miletus.

Tychicus: His name appears twice in the Pastorals (2 Timothy 4:12; Titus 3:12) and also in Acts 20:4; Ephesians 6:21; and Colossians 4:7. He is a beloved brother, faithful minister, and fellow slave of Paul. He, along with Onesimus, transported the letter to the Colossians.

Zenas: Mentioned in Titus 3:13, a Christian man who lived on Crete. Tradition holds that he was later bishop of Lydda in Palestine and the author of *Life of Titus*.

Guide to Pronunciation

Apollos: Ah-POLL-us
Apphia: AP-fee-ah
Archippus: ARCH-ih-puss
Aristarchus: Ar-iss-STAR-kus
Artemas: ARE-teh-mas
Dalmatia: Dal-MAY-shuh
Demas: DEE-mas
Epaphras: Eh-PAH-fras
Ephesus: EH-feh-sus
Erastus: Eh-RASS-tus
Eubulus: YOU-buh-lus
Galatia: Gah-LAY-shuh
Hymenaeus: High-MEEN-ee-us
Jannes: JAH-nus
Jambres: JAM-bres
Linus: LIGH-nus
Marcion: MAR-see-un
Nicopolis: Nih-KAH-poh-lis
Onesimus: Oh-NEH-sih-mus
Philemon: Figh-LEE-mun
Pudens: POO-denz
Thessalonica: Theh-sah-loh-NIGH-kuh
Titus: TIGH-tis
Trophimus: TROH-fih-mus
Tychicus: TIH-kih-kus
Zenas: ZEE-nas

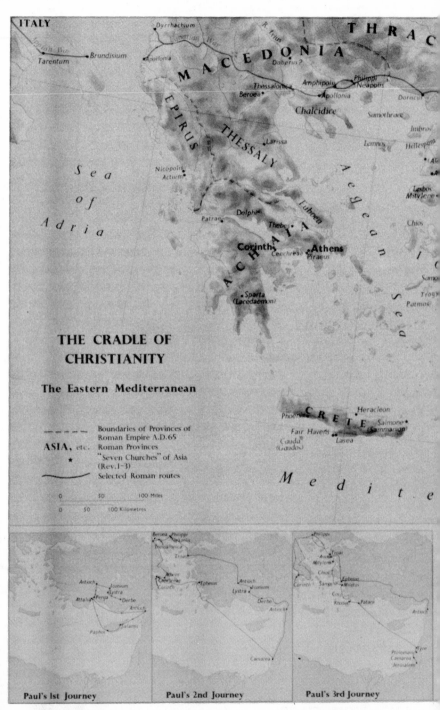

ITALY

Tarentum
Brundisium

Dyrrhachium

MACEDONIA

THRAC

Apollonia

Egnatian Way

R. Trius

Daberus ?

Thessalonica
Beroea

Amphipolis

Apollonia

Philippi
Neapolis

Dorica

EPIRUS

Chalcidice

Samothrace

Imbro

Nicopolis
Actium

THESSALY

Larissa

Lemnos

Hellespo

Ale

A

Sea

of

Adria

Patrae

Delphi
Thebes

Euboea

Lesbos
Mitylene

A
e
g
e
a
n

Chios

Corinth

Cenchreae

Athens
Piraeus

ACHAIA

Sea

Samo

Troge
Patmos

Sparta
(Lacedaemon)

THE CRADLE OF
CHRISTIANITY

The Eastern Mediterranean

CRETE

Heracleon

Phoenix

Fair Havens

Salmone
Hammonium

Cauda
(Gaudos)

Lasea

Boundaries of Provinces of
Roman Empire A.D.65

ASIA, etc.   Roman Provinces

★   "Seven Churches" of Asia
           (Rev.1-3)

Selected Roman routes

0   50   100 Miles

0   50   100 Kilometres

M   e   d   i   t   e

Paul's 1st Journey

Antioch
Iconium
Lystra
Attalia Perga Derbe
Antioch
Paphos
Salamis

Paul's 2nd Journey

Beroea Philippi
Apollonia
Thessalonica
Troas
Athens
Cenchreae
Corinth
Ephesus
Antioch
Lystra Iconium
Derbe
Antioch
Caesarea

Paul's 3rd Journey

Philippi
Assos Troas
Mitylene
Chios
Corinth
Samos Ephesus
Miletus
Cos
Cnidus Patara
Antioch
Ptolemais
Caesarea
Jerusalem
Myra

ASIA MINOR

From the *Oxford Bible Atlas*, Third Edition

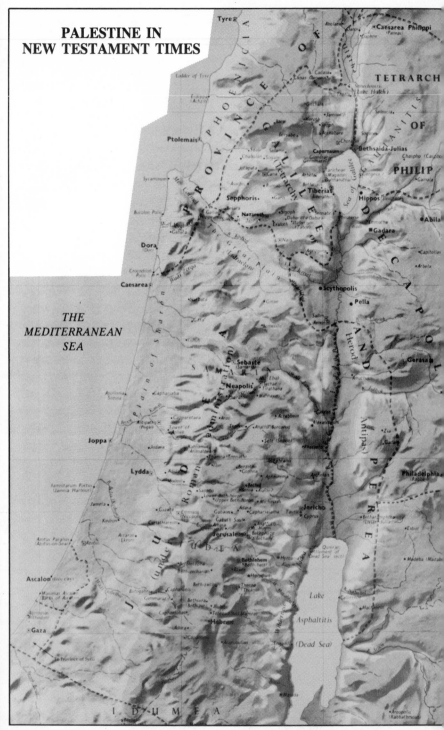

PALESTINE IN
NEW TESTAMENT TIMES

*THE
MEDITERRANEAN
SEA*

From the *Oxford Bible Atlas*, Third Edi